Off Season Pursuits
My pursuits from Alaska to Africa, Australia, New Caledonia and the Amazon

Jake Jacobson
Alaska's Favorite Real Life Wilderness Storyteller

8370 Eleusis Drive, Anchorage, Alaska 99502-4630
books@publicationconsultants.com—www.publicationconsultants.com

ISBN Number: 978-1-59433-511-2
eBook ISBN Number: 978-1-59433-534-1

Library of Congress Number: 2025902784

Copyright © 2025 Jake Jacobson
—First Edition—

All rights reserved, including the right of reproduction in any form, or by any mechanical or electronic means including photocopying or recording, or by any information storage or retrieval system, in whole or in part in any form, and in any case not without the written permission of the author.

Manufactured in the United States of America

During my late grade school years, I became fascinated with the hunting and adventure stories in magazines my father brought home. *True* and *Argosy* were my favorites, with their tales of big game pursuits and intriguing travels to exotic places worldwide. I heard the "call of the wild" in most of those manly stories. But real life in small towns in rural America seemed more like a meek whisper of the mild. I realized early on that I wanted to lead an interesting life full of grand deeds and challenges. If an opportunity for foreign adventure came my way, I was determined to grab it. So began my years of interesting travel about the globe.

Africa 1982

In November 1980, I was in Anchorage on other business, so I attended an Alaska Professional Hunters' Association meeting. A professional hunter from Southern Rhodesia was introduced to all and he had some interesting stories to tell. He mentioned that he had heard about aerial wolf hunting in Alaska, wherein a super cub (PA-18) aircraft would pursue wolves, then, when the right opportunity presented, a shotgunner in the back seat would shoot the running wolves. It proved to be an effective method of wolf management, and the fifty dollar bounty per wolf paid for aviation fuel. The fellow approached me. I thanked him for his suggestion that I bring the aircraft and shotgun to southern Africa, but I told him, though I was intrigued by his proposition, I was much too busy in Alaska. I asked him if the Terrorists he was fighting shot back.... and (heat-seeking missles came to mind and what the bounty was.

In the meantime, my good friend Dr. Bill Gassaway suggested that I contact Peter Johnstone and perhaps work out a trade hunt. Bill was an employee of the Alaska Department of Fish and Game, stationed in Fairbanks. Bill and I had known each other for some time and shared an interest in hunting. Bill had hunted with Johnstone at his Rosslyn concession in Southern Rhodesia and recommended the trip, so I contacted Johnstone. I made it a point to visit with him at the next Safari Club International convention the coming January in Las Vegas.

Johnstone and I maintained a casual acquaintanceship. In early October, 1982, Peter Johnstone sent me a telegram suggesting I come as soon as possible and he could take his end of the trade hunt in 1983, or whenever possible.

Off Season Pursuits

My schedule in Alaska included field trips to provide dental services to residents of three rural villages. before Thanksgiving.

I told Johnstone I would have to think about how I could fulfill my duties in Alaska and fit in a trip of three weeks or more to Rhodesia. After some hurried calculations and communications with the villages, I telegraphed Johnstone that my wife and I would arrive in Rhodesia in early November.

This was a unique opportunity and I did not want to let it pass.

The next day I flew my Super Cub to Point Hope, the largest of the three villages and began working ten to twelve hours each day. When I had completely serviced that village I flew on to Kivalina. Similarly long days in that coastal village saw completion of their normal, contracted, incremental care and I flew on to the last village, Noatak. Five more days of long hours, and I was ready to fly back to Kotzebue. I was tired, but enthused.

Terrorist wars were erupting all over Africa and in the fall of 1982, Peter Johnstone told me all of his American and European booked clients had cancelled, leaving his reservations book completely open. If my wife, Mae, and I could come in November we would have opportunities to take all the different species of trophy we desired - at no fee - on his concession. He would then arrange to come hunt with us in 1983 or even later. And, he had seen one of my 8mm promo films of my Arctic Concession and due to the bad reports from all around Africa causing reluctance to book, he wanted me to put together a promotional 8mm film for his company, Rosslyn Safaris.

So, in the late fall of 1982 Mae, and I went to Zimbabwe/Rhodesia to make a Super eight millimeter promotional movie and trade hunts with Peter Johnstone, owner of Rosslyn Safaris.

AFRICA 1982

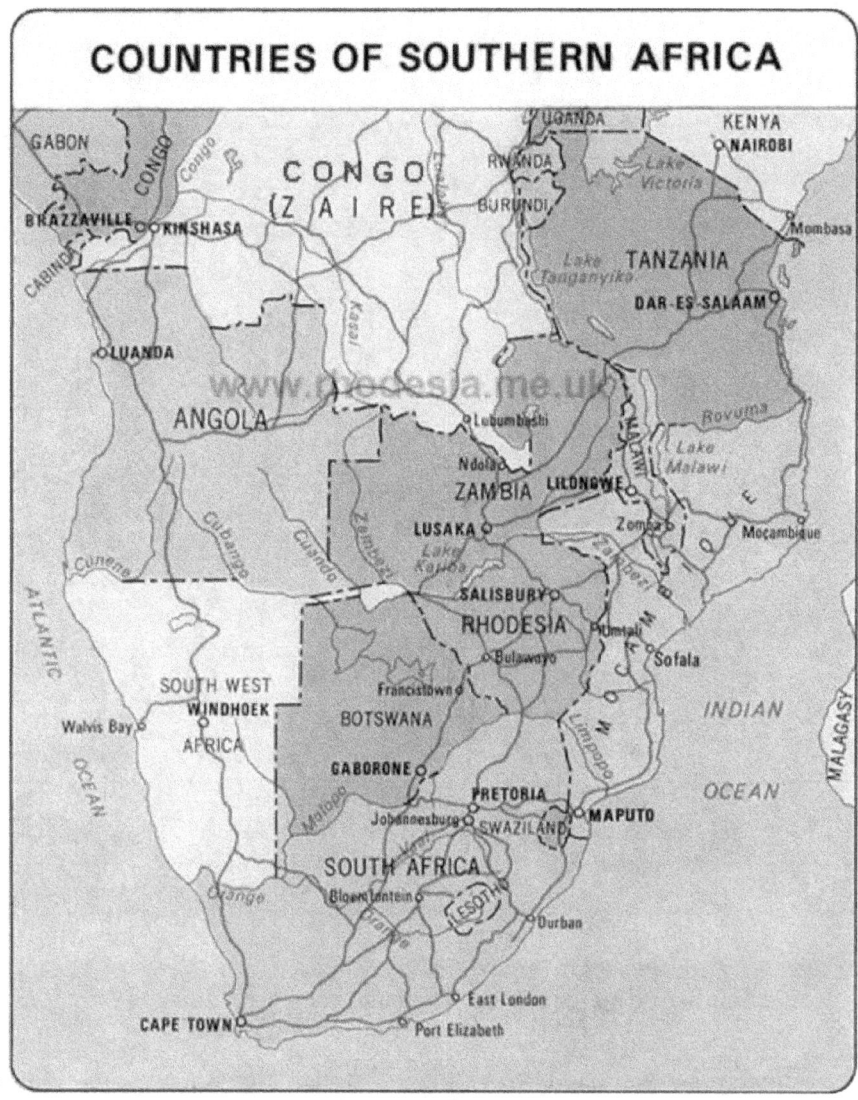

Peter Johnstone's Rosslyn Safaris was headquartered in the Matetsi District (Matabeleland) which was located in the westernmost part of the country, with Zambia to the North, Botswana to the South, and the Caprivi Strip of SouthWest Africa (now called Namibia) immediately to the west. The nearest town to Peter's headquarters was Wankie.

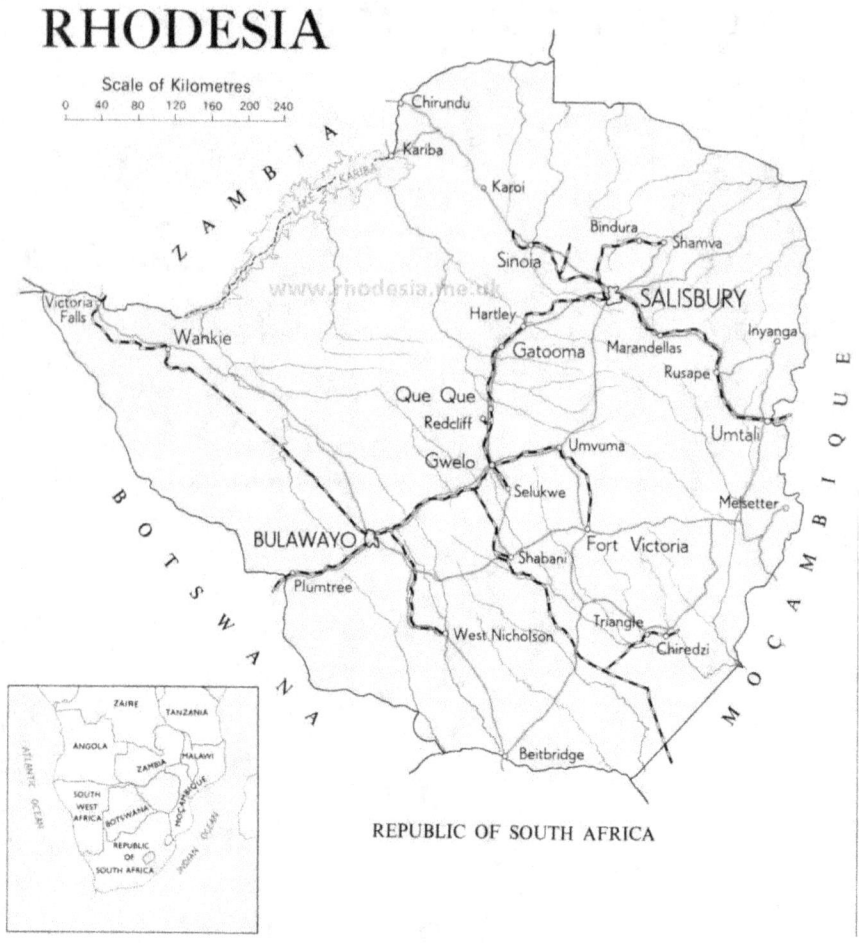

Southern Rhodesia before it became known as Zimbabwe.

The terrorist war had been raging in Rhodesia for several years. Many of the former colonies in Africa were revolting with different tribal factions attempting to take over, and the mood to revolt and become self-governing was contagious. In Southern Rhodesia, the internecine strife was primarily between the Shona and the Matebele, or Ndebele tribes. A political accommodation of sorts had been reached and Robert Mugabe was made president, but roving bands of terrorists were still active. Peter had lost a safari vehicle and two trackers due to land mines that had been laid in the dirt road just outside the outer (second) perimeter fence that surrounded his headquarters. Other farmers and safari operators had similar grim, and all too often deadly experiences. Fatal violence was common. Most sport hunters were not interested in being caught up in such deadly mayhem and were looking for other, safer areas to visit and hunt. The dangerous strife had made booking safaris a very difficult proposition.

Johnstone sent me another telegram saying that all his booked clients had canceled which allowed my wife and me to take all his trophy species at no fee. A brief discussion was sufficient for us to begin making ready for that wonderful, but potentially hazardous opportunity. This was my first opportunity to seek adventure on the dark continent, and we did not want to miss it.

After completing the annual dental visits to three villages, we took a weekend to harvest, butcher, and prepare three bull caribou to leave in our freezer, along with Dall ram and moose meat from guided hunts, ready for us to consume upon our return from Africa. We would not be allowed to bring meat back from any foreign country. My wife, Mae, and I appreciated that we were so blessed to be living in the United States of America, and especially, Alaska.

Our son, Martin worked for Wien Air Alaska, and as his parents, we qualified for non-revenue air travel, in fact, we could upgrade to First Class for very little money, so we did that. It was our first time to fly First Class. Our daughter, Sandy, would mind the store, our house, our six-toed cat, and our dogs which included one Labrador Retriever, Max, and 32 adult huskies.

Passing through Anchorage, on the advice of friends and relatives, we had an attorney friend draw up our wills - just in case.

We made a short stop in Albuquerque, New Mexico to visit my grandmother, Gram, who, at age 83, had spent part of August and September for the past several years, cooking for us at the lodge. Mae did a little shopping in that big city for warm weather clothes and some cold weather coverings to mail back to Kotzebue.

Our journey took us through Amsterdam, then on a KLM jet to Johannesburg, where we spent a night with the wife of a colonel in the South African Defense Force, whom we'd met in Kotzebue. This lady had been touring Alaska and when Mae met her at our store, she invited the South African lady and her friend to our home for dinner. It was not uncommon for Mae to invite interesting strangers to our home, most often for a visit and meal of local fish or game meat. Often these visits resulted in the formation of new and lasting friendships. Such was the case with this lady and her husband.

The next morning we took a South African Airways jet to Victoria Falls, Rhodesia/Zimbabwe, as Southern Rhodesia was by then being called.

Peter Johnstone met us and showed us that remarkable natural wonder, Victoria Falls.

Victoria Falls is a very impressive sight.

Following our brief tour of the falls area, Peter drove us to his carefully chosen Rosslyn Safaris headquarters. On the dirt road just out of the town of Victoria Falls we began to see wild big game close to the roadway. It was amazing to us. We saw wart hogs, zebra, sable antelope, impala, and baboons. When we saw the first giraffe, Mae said "Oh look Jake, a kangaroo !" Well, it may just as well have been a kangaroo. We were completely enthralled!

We stopped to examine a grove of marula trees that had recently been badly damaged by elephants. As we walked about, Mae encountered a large black millipede and called Peter, asking if it was dangerous. He picked it up and allowed it to walk freely across the palm of his hand. He told us it was a Chungalolo, and harmless. He placed it on Mae's bare arm and it tickled her as it climbed up to her shoulder. The weird, but harmless large insect was interesting and entertaining to us.

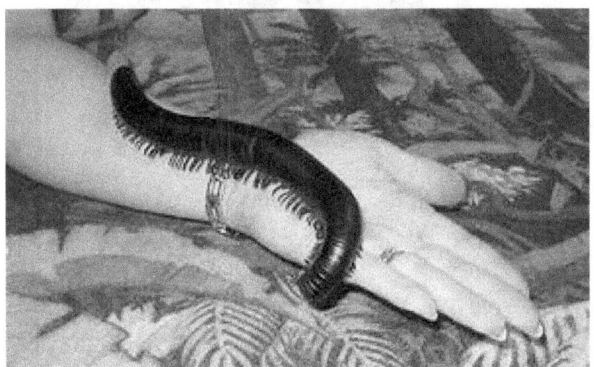

A Chungololo, a type of large, harmless millipede.

A large black Dung Beetle pushing its prize ball of dung with its back legs.

Dung Beetles, a type of Scarab beetle are fascinating little bugs that roll up various types of large animal dung, then deposit their eggs inside. The larvae feed on the dung before hatching. We observed the large black ones, which were nearly large enough to provide decent wing shooting, and also the smaller emerald-colored dung beetles.

The smaller green Dung Bettles were much more eye catching.

We drove by a large, noisy troup of chacma baboons.

Africa 1982

Rosslyn Headquarters on a small hilltop.

Johnstone's headquarters was built on a small knoll of perhaps one hundred feet in height, surrounded by a chain link fence enclosure that protected his garden, chickens, garages, fuel and water storage tanks as well as quarters for his safari and house staff. We drove through the gate and up the hill, then passed through another security gate. The only break in the double chain link fence was topped by concertina razor wire, admitting us to enter the inner circle when a heavy gate was opened. The double fence included a dog run in the middle. He normally kept Rottweilers or Doberman Pinschers there for additional security. He had some land mines available to set in place, in case the dogs were eliminated or disabled by terrorists.

The main kitchen and dining room at Rosslyn

We were greeted by a white gloved house boy in white linen uniform wearing a red, square-topped Fez hat. This was a very formal and impressive, old-style safari operation. It was truly elegant. We were advised that our laundry, including our inexpensive canvas tennis shoes, would be washed each day and that we should ask for any other services we desired. WOW, we didn't offer that degree of service at our lodge in Alaska's Northwest Arctic! Mae really appreciated this high level of personal service.

A properly attired houseboy.

Africa 1982

After freshening up, Peter suggested that we allow him to place our passports and valuables in his safe. We thought that was a good idea and we were shown his strong room. It was a room with thick concrete walls and a heavy steel door. As we left the room, Peter said the safe was securely locked but the outer steel door need not even be closed as none of the black staff would ever dare enter. I questioned that, so he called one of the house staff to us. The man hesitated several feet away, then demurely returned to the bar to prepare gin and tonic cocktails for us.

Seeing my quizzical expression, Peter slightly moved the steel door and a rubber skeleton about a foot long dropped from its suspension and danced crazily on the end of a string. Peter said that the blacks were extremely superstitious and quite frightened by skeletons, whether real or rubber. I told him I had more faith in the locked steel safe, than I had in any primitive superstitions.

There was time to sight in the rifles that Peter had for us, a 30:06 and a .375, so we did that. Neither rifle needed adjustment. Mae did not shoot the larger caliber gun. As the sun dropped on the horizon, we noticed that we quickly became chilly.

The trackers wore heavy, knit wool caps. I've always found that to be common, but strangely curious behavior by blacks, in hot weather.

We enjoyed our cocktails followed by a sumptuous meal of some type of local antelope, young wart hog, homegrown vegetables, and a sweet dessert.

After hearing many stories and cautionary tales, it was time to sleep, as we planned to rise well before sunup. Peter escorted us to our private hut. We were advised to never leave our private quarters after dark without a "torch" (flashlight) in hand, because spitting cobras frequented the buildings as they searched for rodents, and the snakes would not be comfortable with us at close quarters .... nor would we be comfortable with them. All cobras have neurotoxic venom and their bite is most often fatal.

During our three-week stay, we encountered spitting cobras on several occasions. Once, early one morning we found one in the middle of a primitive dirt road, or track, as the locals call them. Rosslyn's Chief Professional Hunter, Roy Vincent, kicked sand at the snake which rose with its hood expanded, and spit venom at him. Though he wore eyeglasses, he shielded them with his hand and showed me the venom on the back of his hand. Those Elapid snakes spit with deadly accuracy, and if the venom reaches its target - the victim's eyes - great pain and possible blindness result. Most spitting cobras' venom/toxin is significantly cytotoxic, apart from the neurotoxic and cardiotoxic effects typical of other cobra species. They can spit their venum up to three meters away. I captured that accurate spitting action on the movie camera, but Peter insisted that I not use it for the promotional film. It would alarm some potential hunters.

Spitting Cobra in action.

AFRICA 1982

Peter and Roy Vincent, warned us to never depart the hilltop inner fences - no matter what - as throughout Africa, most whites were murdered by blacks who served as staff members. This violence all began with the Mau-mau uprising in Tanganyika, then spread to Kenya, and now was rampant in Southern Rhodesia and other former colonies. The "Africanization of Africa" was supported by naive and inexperienced liberals around the world.

Regarding that timely bit of advice, one night about two o'clock in the morning, my wife and I awoke to the sound of a horn blaring on one of the safari vehicles. I slipped on my britches, grabbed a "torch" and went outside. The noise from the horn was loud and continuous. I thought the electrical drain on the battery might keep us from our intended trip the next day, but then, I remembered Roy's warning and stopped short. What a good way to get someone to go to the garage, there to be ambushed and perhaps filleted. I returned to our hut and after a few minutes, the noise stopped. I never did find out if some staff member had fixed it, or perhaps had set it up. Curiously neither Peter nor Roy heard the noise.

On the first hunting day, we drove to a part of the Rosslyn concession near Hwange (Wankie) Park. That area had not been visited by Peter or Roy in several months, so we were checking on what game might be found there. We saw a black rhino bull early in the morning which paid no attention to us. Rhinos were not on the list of available game in that area. After leaving the vehicle we trekked through the dry desert bush country, encountering a black mamba which rapidly slithered away. We saw several types of hornbills (birds) and many game animals.

An ever observant Hornbill

Early in the afternoon, we came upon a large group of cape buffalo. I noticed that all seemed to have several tick birds or oxpeckers on their back or heads which were busily feeding on external parasites - ticks. The huge wild bovines spotted us just as we saw them and about sixty bulls came trotting up to inspect us more closely. Roy was with us and I noticed that he kept his rifle slung and did not chamber a round, so I followed his example. The buffalo formed a semicircle in front of us and began to advance. They would stop, then one brave bull would come a few steps closer and the rest would follow. Their display reminded me of teenage boys, daring each other. This advance and stand maneuver was repeated several times until the buffalo were about fifty yards from us. Mae and I were glancing around for a tree. Roy remained calm and stood still. As the animals began another advance, Roy pulled out his handkerchief and waved it above his head, as he shouted, "Go away you bloody caffirs," The Latin name for Cape Buffalo is *Syncerus caffer*. (Caffer is a derogatory Arabic term for unbelievers.) The huge beasts swung their heads to the left and charged off and away from us to the great relief of Mae and me.

Africa 1982

A band of curious bulls.

We often saw Oxpecker birds feeding on ticks of buffalo, rhino, hippos, zebra, and other large herbivores. The name Oxpecker refers to two species of small parasite-eating birds from Africa. It does not refer to an anatomical feature of any animal and it is not a synonym for "bull whanger."

We saw Sable and Roan antelope and many other species of big game that day. It seemed we'd arrived at a hunter's paradise

A bull Sable

A pair of Roan antelope

Early the next morning we started off with Roy and two trackers in quest of that same herd of buffalo, as Roy said he saw at least two in the bunch that he figured were worthy of closer scrutiny. We located them about two miles from where we'd seen them the day before and after nearly an hour of maneuvering to locate a trophy-class bull, Roy said, "Jake, there he is and he's bigger than I had thought, better try to anchor him, as they are getting twitchy." After another half hour of stalking, I had an opportunity for a clear shot and fed the bull a 300-grain lead pellet from the .375 Holland and Holland. The first shot into the withers staggered the bull, but it took another round to put him down. He was a dandy, with huge bosses and over forty inches of horn length. I might not have easily picked him out, surrounded as he was by many other big bulls. When hunting wild game with which you are unfamiliar, it makes sense to have an experienced guide.

Mae and me with the big bull.

After taking pictures I went to a puddle to rinse the mud and blood from my hands. As I was about to dip into the muddy stagnant water, Roy said to stay clear. He motioned for me to come to the safari car and use drinking water for cleaning up, as any bush water, especially if stagnant, was apt to carry Bilharzia, or Schistosomiasis, also known as snail fever, or Katayama fever, is a disease caused by parasitic flatworms called schistosomes. This is a disease condition caused by parasitic trematode flatworms which one should avoid, lest the worms cause severe illness or even death.

Roy and I, with the two trackers, used an electric come-a-long winch to get the huge bull loaded into the back of the Toyota land cruiser. As we drove back to the hilltop at Rosslyn we saw several species of antelope and three of the seemingly ubiquitous wart hogs.

Peter said this Cape Buffalo ranked SCI #44 in 1982.

A medium-sized male Warthog

Immediately upon driving up to the butchering facility, local staff hung the carcass and began to skin and quarter it. Most of the meat was cut into strips, then brined and hung to dry for biltong (jerky), which is quite tasty and keeps well in the hot conditions of Africa. By law, the hunting concession owns the meat of all wild game taken by their guests and everything is put to its best use. Much of the meat is sold to locals.

Local staff eat primarily "sudza" - a very "thick porridge" made from finely ground white cornmeal popularly known as mealie meal. It is similar to polenta but thicker in texture, and it is usually served as a main dish. I found it to be uninteresting, even after flavoring with steak sauce, etc.

A smaller female warthog was shot for dinner and Leopard bait. Peter, Mae, Roy and two "boys" with the female "bait wart hog" which also provided us with a tasty supper. After washing up, with gin in hand, Mae and I walked down the hill to watch the processing, all of which was quickly and efficiently done. The blacks on Peter's staff were experienced and efficient in their jobs.

Before dark we were called back up the hill for dinner. I noticed one of the staff skinners looking at me as he sliced through the cuts of meat and wondered if he would like to do me the same way. I wondered if he might be the one who had set the horn to blaring the previous night.

Mae was happy with her large Warthog.

I enjoyed having the occasional cigar in those days and had brought along two boxes of fifty smokes each. I noticed that the trackers were rolling plain dry, brown grass up in newspaper and smoking it like a giant cigarette. I figured that had to be a really hot smoke, so, after an especialy difficult tracking of a wounded antelope, I gave one of my factory cigars to each man. My gifts seemed to excite them. I'd noticed Roy observing and later I asked him privately if my simple generosity was okay. He said it was okay, but that I should never forget that even though some of the blokes smiled a lot and spoke what seemed to be our language, few of them shared our values and that I should be ever aware of that fact. I was reminded of the hostile looks I'd detected from the fellow butchering the buffalo.

Africa 1982

The camp at Katherine.

Peter had a Cessna 206 aircraft which is common in Alaska, but was a rarity in Africa. He flew us to another concession called Katherine. On that flight, we saw more Black Rhinos, many Giraffes, and hundreds of antelope of several species.

There was a good number of elephants around the Katherine property, so Peter offered me the opportunity to shoot one. The government fee was $2,000. I told him I would shoot one if the ivory could be sold for that amount. I had several Wooly Mammoth tusks at home, and ivory can become a bit of a burden to maintain. Ivory must be prevented from cracking, etc. I had no great desire to kill an elephant or collect the ivory. We looked over three different groups in as many locations but did not find one of an estimated sixty pounds or more per side, so I did not shoot one, but I greatly enjoyed the search. I have never regretted my decision.

Nevertheless, it was exciting to stalk those huge pachyderms and I did get some good movie footage from very close range. Most elephants are shot at close range, often at well under fifty yards and nearly all are taken with heart shots. The brain shots as often shown in movies are seldom permitted by professional hunters, because the brain is small, and too many attempts to hit it result in wounding which can lead to really dangerous situations, as well as long follow-ups of the wounded beast.

After securing the airplane, we drove around in the safari vehicle, looking over the game and searching for spoor. A large leopard had left plenty of tracks, so Mae shot a female warthog, and it was hung high in a tree as bait.

The first morning in Katherine opened with a troop of baboons coming into the yard on a raiding party. Roy said I should shoot one of the big males, so I did. Those monkeys are very impressive animals with a huge set of canines - sufficient to give a leopard cause for concern.

The large male Baboon led his troop into the camp.

"Jake, you've shot the gardener," Peter hollered when the big male baboon dropped.

Mae rushed out to see what had happened, only to be relieved that Peter was making a joke.

AFRICA 1982

A dandy example of a Common Reedbuck, taken
incidentally to another animal's stalk - Peter scored all trophies
and told me it placed #12 in the SCI record book.

As we returned to the camp Roy pointed out a Kori Bustard. This turkey sized bird has become rare in many parts of southern Africa but we spotted three individuals during our three weeks of hunting. They are the largest Bustard and one of the world's heaviest flying birds. The males are larger than the females

A Kori Bustard, reportedly excellent table fare.

In the meantime, we had a large selection of species and numbers of big game animals to hunt. The Common Reedbuck pictured previously, placed number twelve in the Safari Club International record book in 1982. As we stalked the reedbuck I was reminded of American mule deer by the size, appearance, and behavior of that species.

Leopards seem to prefer spoiled or even maggot-ridden baits. These conditions are quick to develop in Africa.

A leopard had visited our hanging bait hog, and Roy expected it to return at dusk, so late that afternoon he and Mae sat in a blind, as Peter and I looked over more elephants. About a half hour before dark, I heard a single shot and told Peter that I'd wager that Mae had shot her leopard.

When Peter and I got to the blind, Roy asked her if she was sure she hit it well, and she confirmed that she thought it was a heart shot. A tracker with a shotgun was seated on the hood of the land cruiser, Peter drove and Roy occupied the other front seat. Wounded leopards injure more people than any others of the "Big Five" and African Professional Hunters take minimal chances on a client being scratched or bitten by one of those aggressive big cats.

We drove less than one hundred yards through the long grass when the tracker whooped, stood up, and pointed excitedly. The cat was lying dead just beneath the bumper. Mae had made a heart shot.

AFRICA 1982

Mae is likely the only Eskimo woman ever to kill a leopard in Rhodesia.

Mae and me with her excellent Sable.

Mae shot a very good Sable antelope at Katherine and we saw many Roans, but they were protected, so we just filmed and appreciated the opportunity to see them.

It was another magic day for us! At my insistence, we cooked some of the leopard meat, as I knew from experience that lynx, bobcat, and puma were lean and delicious. That African feline cooked well done was fine eating, too. I recall that Peter and Roy were not interested in eating any of the cat meat.

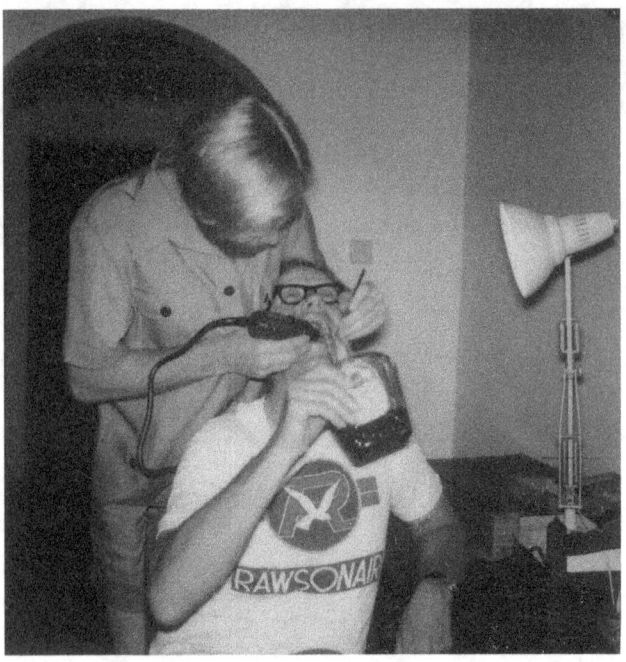

Using a Dremel Tool to remove the sharp edge off a chipped tooth for Peter Johnstone with whisky anesthetic.

I carried emergency dental equipment on all such trips and did perform a few tooth extractions while in Hwange and, later, in other places. Aids was not commonly heard of yet and I did not routinely wear rubber gloves. Luckily, I did not contract any communicable diseases on any of my five trips to Africa, - but I was definitely smitten by love and fascination with the African bush and its bountiful wild game.

Rosslyn and Katherine camps kept a large number of domestic chickens for eggs and meat. I grew up around domestic chickens for our own use and every safari camp had chickens. I've always loved the sound of a rooster crowing and even today, when I hear a rooster, I am immediately reminded of my childhood, and of Africa.

Many times we encountered Vervet monkeys.
The males display a striking blue scrotum.

We flew back to Rosslyn, then accompanied Peter to Hwange town to purchase chicken feed, and other supplies, and to get his mail. I noticed several pairs of men walking hand in hand and asked Peter if they were homosexuals, or what? He said that holding hands was a common practice for men in that area and that behavior did not necessarily indicate they were homosexuals.

In the post office was a large sign that stated: "IF A PERSON SHOULD CALL YOU 'KAFFIR' YOU MIGHT SMITE HIM". Kaffir is an Arabic term meaning "unbeliever", but has been used for centuries as a derogatory term for blacks. The Latin name for Cape Buffalo is *Kaffir, kaffir syncereus* or *Syncerus caffer,* a true black unbeliever, I reckoned.

During a relief (Pee) break I found this tortoise that looked similar to the desert tortoises found in Arizona.

Local names for blacks include wog, boogie, blue gum, coon, sooty, smoke, jigaboo, jungle bunny, jig, jit, spade, and spook. I suspect there are many other derogatory terms, as well, and likely no fewer negative terms, or epithets for whites.

We drove west one day to a place called Pandamatenga, where we encountered a herd of more than 80 elephants. At one point we were approached by a medium-sized bull, which Peter thought was showing signs of being aggressive. We three got underneath the land cruiser and the elephant walked to within 10 feet of us, apparently checking out the vehicle. Then the bull faded into the bush.

Roy and Rene Vincent and their two children, Alan and Diana, accompanied us to the Zambezi River to see more of the country and do some fishing. As we drove down from the foothills toward the great river, the road was blocked by some of Mugabe's soldiers, potentially members of the notorious Fifth Brigade. As Roy slowed the vehicle, he handed me a .45 pistol and said I should stuff it into a space on the inside of the seat and have it handy, just in case it was needed. Armed men stood on each side of our car and did not act at all friendly.

Not one smiled. After a few minutes of conversation between Roy and the group's leader in the Ndebele language, we were allowed to continue down the road toward the river. It gave all of us an uneasy feeling to be stopped and questioned in such an aggressive manner by scowling people who were so well-armed and seemed so primitive, with unsmiling, aggressive faces and demeanors. I got the impression that they hated us and probably hated all white people.

Our only catch of the day, was this medium Tiger Fish.

That part of the Zambezi River had a healthy population of large Nile crocodiles, and we saw several that day. We also saw several dugout vessels with minimal freeboard, powered by blacks using paddles. They were fishing, I assumed. We caught only one medium-sized Tiger fish and drove back to the Rosslyn headquarters.

We saw lions on at least five occasions. I'm sure lions saw us more frequently. With two trackers in the bed of the safari truck, when one of them saw a Lion he would slap the top of the cab to alert us, then both men would lie down below the side rails, in hopes that the Lions would not come after them. Lions were known to have jumped into the back of trucks and grab people, usually with bloody, often fatal consequences.

Roy led me to this Grevy's zebra, part of which was used for lion bait. This male shows shadow stripes.

We tied a rope to the entrails of zebra and antelope on several occasions and dragged them behind the safari car to leave a scent trail for lions and we filled buckets with blood and gore and scattered the contents about. We placed bloodshot and otherwise unusable meat in locations to attract Lions, but never did we find an adult male at the baits, or on our foot treks. Several lionesses and cubs visited the baits, but all of the prides seemed to lack male partners.

AFRICA 1982

Two lionesses, squinting in the sun light.

Mae shot several fine Southern Impala rams.

I noticed that if we spooked game during our stalk, most animals would run a relativelly short distance, permitting another stalk after a few minutes. In the wild places I've hunted in Alaska and other states, once spooked, most game was gone for the day.

As is the common practice in Africa and Australia, many of the open grassy areas were set afire to burn off the old grass, which encourages new green growth to sprout. The local acacia thorn bush, knob thorn trees, and other medium-sized trees were resistant to the burning.

One evening, as we were driving back to Rosslyn headquarters we sighted two large male Lions lying in the middle of a small, recently burned grassland. The manes of both were long enough to cover their ears, indicating they were five years old or older. Roy drove the truck to within 80 meters of them, causing them to stand up and calmly look our way. He said, "Jake, they're both good males, shoot whichever one you want."

Just at dusk we found 2 large male lions in a burned meadow near the road.

I got out with my movie camera and said that I intended to shoot them both, but not with a rifle unless it proved to be necessary. That would have been too ignominious an end to such a magnificent animal. I got several minutes of close-up movie footage before the pair walked into the thorn bush and out of sight. So, neither Mae nor I shot a lion. Nor was either of us upset about that. I would not enjoy having to tell how we merely drove up to such an impressive beast and shamelessly shot it.

Never before had I seen so many species of big game animals so readily available to hunt.

Rosslyn headquarters was many miles from any river or large lake, but a single hippo had taken up residence in a small pond near the main house. We often watched it mornings and evenings.

The lone local hippo appeared early and late each day.

When a large herd of Livingstone's Eland moved onto a neighbor's concession, we were given permission to use his area to hunt. After glassing dozens of the huge antelope I shot a good-sized bull after Mae said she would not care to shoot the .375.

A good, mature Livingstone Eland bull.

As we were looking over some new territory one day we came upon a group of Waterbuck. Roy said that one was a very good bull, so without much hesitation, after a forty-minute stalk, I shot what looked like the best one.

An exceptional Waterbuck, taken incidental to another pursuit.

To my way of thinking, the Greater Kudu is the most impressive antelope in all of Africa. It is also one of the most common of the antelope, but we had many frustrations in our attempts to collect one. Finally, an opportunity at a decent Kudu was presented and I was able to take it. I believe more graceful and better-eating big game animal cannot be found.

AFRICA 1982

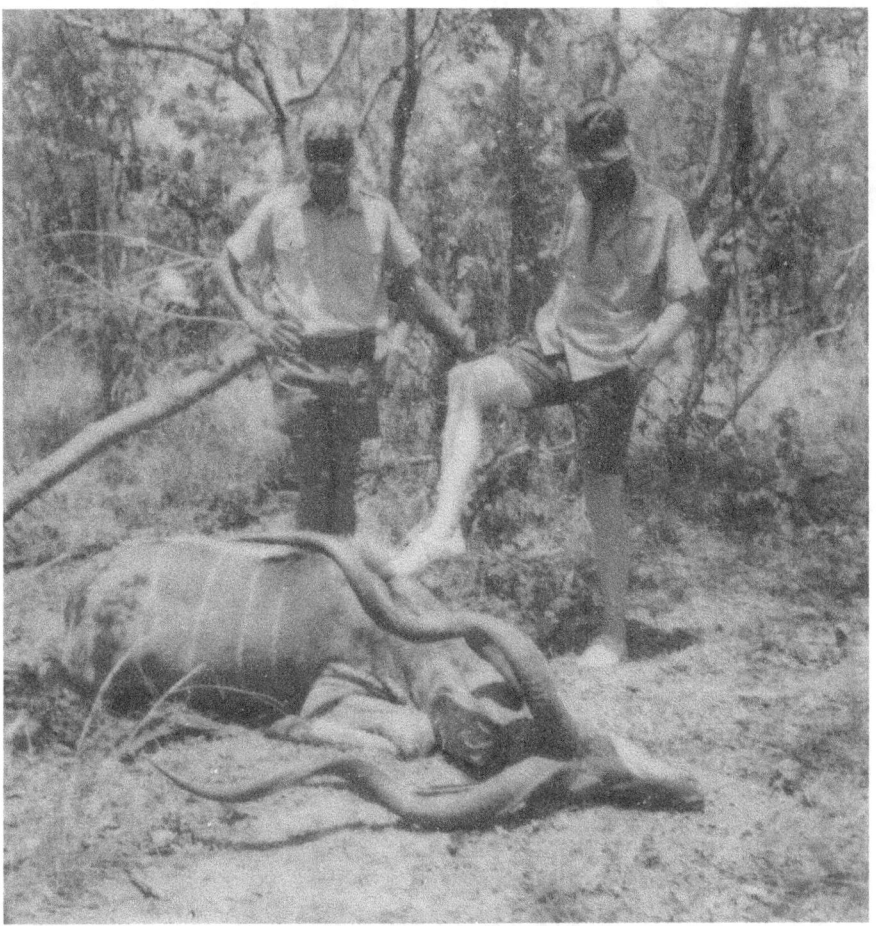

Finally, a Greater Kudu bull.

Just three days before our scheduled departure, as we approached the Rosslyn headquarters we came upon a clan of Spotted (Laughing) Hyenas, and in the dim light of advancing dusk, I shot one of the adult males. The female spotted hyenas are larger than the males and theirs is a matriarchal society.

The shot was made in dense underbrush as the animal sprinted away. I felt lucky to collect this unique trophy.

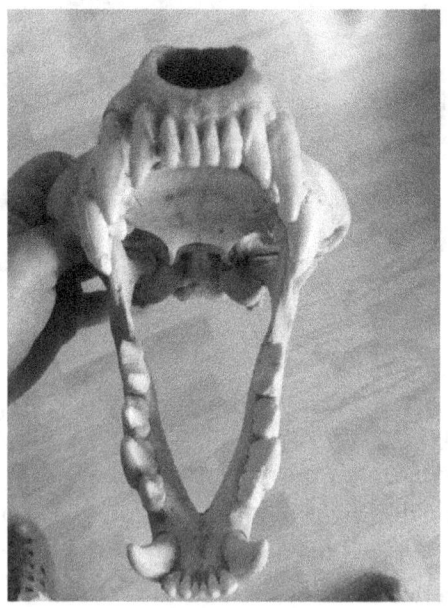

I wanted to see the teeth and overall dental arrangement that enabled Hyenas to crush the long bones of animals as large as the Cape Buffalo. Hyenas have no grinders - only shearing teeth. Wolverines have similar dentition.

AFRICA 1982

A Common, or Gray Duiker taken near the headquarters.

Life is full of surprises and no less so in the African bush than elsewhere. As we began a several mile trek to return to the headquarters just in front of us appeared a mature Kudu bull. Roy told me it was not quite as large as the one I had recently taken, but he approved of me collecting this fine trophy. This animal seemed not so alert and twitchy as is common to the species. After a short stalk the bull offered me a clear shot and I put it down.

Kudu normally do not come so easily as this one.

We observed colorful African Hunting Dogs on several occasions. They are fascinating to watch, but our times with them were brief. I did not attempt to shoot one.

At Rosslyn headquarters with some of the 22 animals we had taken.

Mae and I departed Victoria Falls with many unique and wonderful memories. We dreamed of someday operating a safari service in that area, perhaps during the long Alaskan winters. Land was available at about thirty-five cents an acre, but the political situation was worse than tenuous, and that kept us from seriously considering movng to the dark continent.

Our inexpensive first-class flight home was a wonderful topper to the greatest trip we had done together.

As we discussed the horrible changes taking place in colonial Africa, we saw aboriginal claims and preferences being aired and acted upon in Alaska. The subsistence issue was dividing Alaskans and other Americans, but as it gained force non-subsistence qualifying citizens were losing their equal rights to fish, game, and all other natural resources. That is unconstitutional, divisive, criminal, and truly a grievous pity! The world is in the throes of liberal turmoil and getting crazier by the day as the human population increases!

The agreement between Peter and me was that Mae and I would got to Rhodesia/Zimbabwe to hunt and put together a short 8mm promotional move for Roslyn Safaris in November 1982. The timing was important because all of Peter's booked clients for that year had cancelled due to the terrorist activity. So in December I got right to work cutting and splicing together a short film for Peter.

He would come to Alaska to hunt in September 1983. However, Peter was unable to join us in 1983, and in September 1983, Mae suddenly and tragically passed away. We re-scheduled Peter to come to hunt in September 1984. Dr. Bill Gasaway, who the year before had suggested that a trade hunt with Peter might be a wonderful thing for both of us. I invited Bill to come along for Peter's hunt. Bill was the chief moose biologist for the Alaska Department of Fish and Game, based in Fairbanks. He and I had hunted together previously and he had hunted with Peter in Rhodesia. Bill was pleased to come for Peter's Alaskan hunt. Bill brought his own SuperCub and his notable skill at calling moose for the hunt.

I had scheduled only Peter Johnstone for the two week booking of Aug.30 to Sept.12, so the three of us enjoyed the experience without other guests. Peter was interested in fishing as well, so I flew him down to the Noatak River to catch some fall-run Arctic Char. We were successful with fishing and on the way back to the lodge we flew over a string of caribou numbering about sixty animals, which included one outstanding bull. In less than one hour, Peter had the truly magnificent Caribou on the ground.

Peter Johnstone with his superb bull Caribou.

In 1984 it was legal to shoot a caribou the same day the hunter was airborne, so early in the booking when the opportunity came, Peter collected one of the finest Barren Gound Caribou I have ever seen.

I had been watching a huge bull moose near the lodge for more than a week. I hoped for, but could not find a better trophy, so when Bill Gasaway called the moose onto my eighty acres of private property, Peter shot it. This moose placed number three in the 1984 Safari Club International and the Alaska Professional Hunters annual competition.

Peter enjoyed the fresh baked Arctic Char so much I took him back to the Noatak River for more fish. As we flew downstream I noticed some big bull moose resting at the base of an old river cutbank not far downstream from the lodge. The moose seemed tired after a prolonged period of rutting activities.

Peter Johnstone is a big fellow, as was his moose.

With our first two casts, we landed two nice female char, each of which measured a bit over thirty inches in length. That was enough for a nice dinner and a large salmon spread for sandwiches the next day, so we got back in the cub and returned to the lodge. I flew over the cut bank where the moose had selected to rest and we saw what I believed to be the largest grizzly I had ever seen standing over a recently killed bull moose. I banked the aircraft and flew over the scene again. Yes, that was the biggest grizzly I had ever seen. It looked more like a Kodiak Brown Bear than an interior grizzly.

Not wanting to bugger the great bear away from its kill, I turned for the lodge. We would return late the next afternoon and attempt to harvest this great bruin after an overnight sleep in my tent.

The next day was spent leisurely until we loaded the cub about five o'clock in the evening. We were only a few minutes flying time from the bear and I found a gravel bar to land and sleep on which was about a twenty minute walk from the site. We made no fire that night, but I brought a thermos of coffee from the lodge for the morning.

We were both awake before daylight. We enjoyed a cup of coffee and some "Bearclaw" pastries before walking to the kill site.

Peter asked me how many bears I had been directly involved with taking. I told him about one hundred forty. He replied," Oh, one never takes a hundred lions wthout at least one mauling.

I told Peter that all bears are extremely dangerous and strong and to keep that in mind as we cautiously approached the huge beast. We should give the huge Grizzly no less respect than we would offer a lion. I also mentioned for the second time to not shoot the bear in the head, as that might make record book entry impossible, and this animal clearly would place high in the book.

The underbrush was thick, but I knew exactly where the bear should be. As we crept closer I recognized the right ear of the bear and pointed it out to Peter. We were approximately thirty yards from the kill site, and the bruin.

Silently the bear raised up on its front legs to see us and I whispered to Peter, "Shoot now!"

Peter's bullet struck the bear in the throat and it dropped down with its head on its front paws. Before I could stop him, Peter put another bullet in the top of the bear's skull.

The grizzly squared 8 feet, 10 inches.

We were both elated and relieved. Peter told me he was thinking of my reminder that grizzlies are dangerous and decided to make sure it was dead with the second shot. That was a pity as the skull was damaged beyond elgibility for record book measurement. It's dimensions exceeded 27.5 inches.

We took our time with skinning, removing all the subcutaneous fat to minimize weight, though the huge hide still weighed a bit over one hundred pounds, but we still were ready to fly to the lodge by two o'clock that afternoon. Upon seeing the hide and skull, Bill Gasaway was as elated as we.

Peter's ram was a dandy.

I'd been watching a band of 5 rams on a spine east of the lodge that we called Middle Mountain. Both Gasaway and I reckoned the two best rams to be a bit less than forty inches on the curl, but they were takers, unless we could locate a larger one. Peter's time was running out and

I wanted to get him out in the float plane for a look at some different country and maybe collect a black bear.

So, just after daybreak the next day Peter and I were off for the ram. The day was cool and nearly windless as we trudged up the steep slope. We could see the lodge every step of the way. A bit before ten that morning Peter had his pick of the sheep and he shot a dandy. It measured 38 and 5/8 inches on each horn. Neither horn was broomed.

We were back inside the lodge by three that afternoon. I never before had a guest take four trophies that matched of the superb quality of these.

The next day we closed up the lodge and as we flew to Kotzebue we passed over several thousand caribou heading south for their winter range.

Peter Johnstone and 3 of his 4 outstanding trophies.

I had time and wanted to take Peter in the float plane, but he was anxious about possibly missing his return flight home, so the black bear hunt did not take place.

This was my first trade hunt. I wish all trades worked out so satisfactorily for both parties.

I made four more trips to hunt and/or film in Africa, but none were so wonderful as this first one.

Australia's "Top End"

For several years I had read stories and seen photographs of hunting Giant Rusa deer on the island of New Caledonia. I was attracted to the animal and the French-controlled island where they were most commonly hunted.

My good friend Bob Penfold was running some hunts in New Caledonia and he asked if I might be interested in going there to make a promotional video for him. As soon as I could recover from my surprise, I answered in the positive. That was in January 1990.

As travel to that part of the world is expensive, we planned for me to do an additional video on buffalo hunting in Australia's "top end" in early July, then head back to his home in Newcastle. From there we would fly to Noumea, New Caledonia, and spend a couple of weeks or so hunting and filming Rusa deer.

But Bob informed me in May that due to local native (Kanak) social unrest, the French government in New Caledonia decided to restrict the importation of all firearms and ammunition. So our plans were put on indefinite hold. That was disappointing to me, but as I had been delayed in the process of having my float plane's fabric replaced, it turned out for the best that I was not absent from Alaska that summer.

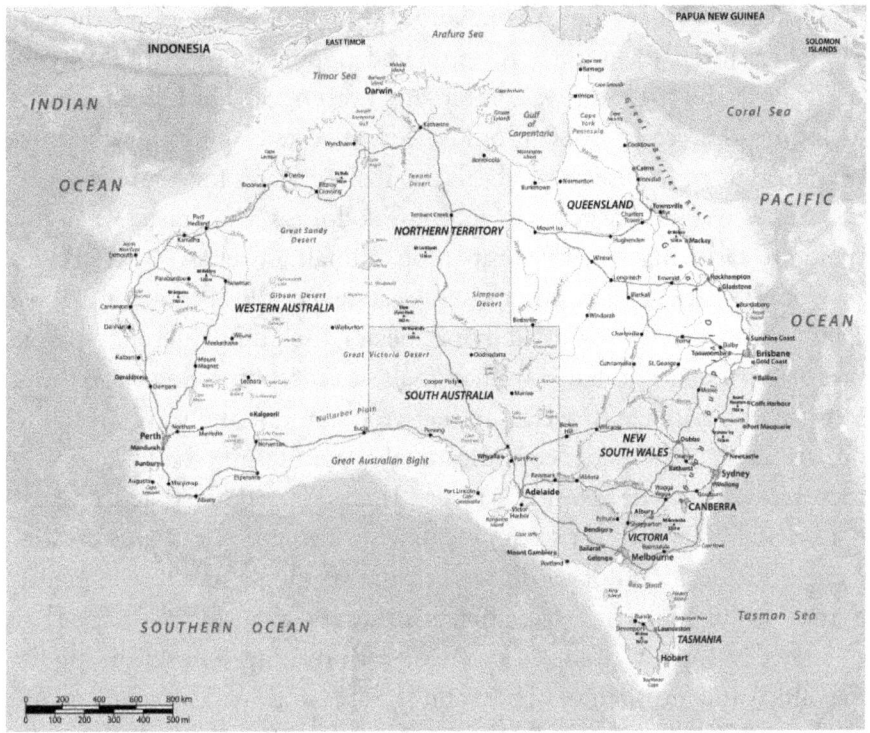

The Australian continent.

By January of 1991, Bob had arranged for rifles to rent from local French farmers in New Caledonia and had learned that small amounts of ammunition could be brought into the territory, so long as they were counted by the admitting officers. Upon departure from New Caledonia, the number of live rounds and spent cartridge cases would again be counted and must match the number of live rounds brought in by each person. Bob would see to supplying forty rounds of ammunition for the .243 rifles. We could not afford many missed shots.

So I departed Kotzebue on July 1. I lost July 2 due to crossing the International Date Line and arrived in Sidney at 5:30 am of Wednesday, July 3. The official time was eighteen hours later than Kotzebue. I soon boarded a jet bound for Darwin with a stop in Alice Springs, where we set our watches back one-half hour. Adjusting watch time by a half hour was a new one for me.

I learned that the Australian government's Dingo eradication program kicked in, due to an estimated population of 13,000 of the wild dogs. The program was employing every means of killing Dingos, including the use of 1080 (Sodium Fluoroacetate) poison, which had been forbidden for use throughout the United States for many years.

Sodium Fluoroacetate is colorless, odorless, and tasteless and is therefore easily ingested by companion animals as well as native species. Its victims – intended or otherwise – experience a slow, agonizing death. 1080 is considered toxic to all living species, including microbes, plants, insects, birds, and humans. In mammals, it causes birth defects, reduced fertility, and damage to the reproductive system, brain, heart, and other organs. Anecdotal evidence indicates that its use may be linked to an increased risk of developing cancer. There are reports that the Nazis considered using this poison on Jewish prisoners in concentration camps but decided not to do so, because of the danger to the guards. Symptoms include vomiting, anxiety, disorientation, and shaking. These quickly develop into frenzied behavior with running and screaming fits, drooling, uncontrolled twitches, and seizures, followed by total collapse and death. This agony may go on for up to 48 hours. Furthermore, once an animal dies from 1080, animals that eat its carcass will also die. This goes on for several systems, killing birds and even insects that eat contaminated carcasses.

The fourth of July is just another day to Australians. Bob bought us breakfast in Darwin, then we loaded his two Toyota Land Cruisers and drove to Katherine where we purchased groceries and other supplies. Our lunch was the Aussie favorite - meat pies and chips (French fries). That was "fair dinkum tucker, down under, mate". I noticed again how similar Australians are to Americans, however, we are somewhat separated by the common language.

We headed down the road for the Mountain Valley headquarters (or cattle station) of John Harrower, from whence the buffalo hunts would be conducted. The dirt roads made for a powdery dusting of everything and everyone. No one escaped the "Darwin suntan".

After about an hour of driving, the engine of my vehicle suddenly began to throw billows of smoke from under the hood, so I blared my horn to alert Bob and pulled to the side of the road. A water hose had become disconnected, so I put it back in place, cinched down the hose clamp, which luckily was still on the hose, and resumed the drive, but it soon blew off again. Bob figured we'd better take the rig back to Katherine for a new hose and whatever other repairs were necessary, so we hooked it up to his vehicle and began towing it back to town.

About a mile down the road we were pulled over by two policemen who were a bit testy, but nevertheless courteous in demeanor over some minuscule departure from towing regulations. They took Bob to town for repair parts. I remained with the vehicles. Bob soon returned, and we re-rigged the tow and drove on to Katherine.

We transferred freight from the disabled Toyota to a Ford station wagon, found some fast food chicken to stuff down our necks, and drove on to Mountain Valley, arriving after midnight and completely tired out. En route I saw a couple of large snakes, which I could not identify on the road. At dusk two feral pigs darted across the road in front of me and, once darkness descended upon us, many sets of eyes glowing in the headlights, owned I assumed, by Dingos, Kangaroos or feral pigs. This dry, dusty country seemed to be well populated by interesting, but, to me, unknown life forms.

July 5 We were drinking some morning starting fluid (coffee for me and black tea for Bob) to greet the sun at 7:00 am. It dawned clear and warm.

Hundreds of white-headed Galahs were having a fly-in convention near the buildings. Responding to some chirping in the bathroom, I discovered a couple dozen chartreuse-colored green frogs in the toilet tank. I suppose they kept other forms of life in the tank and bowl to a minimum.

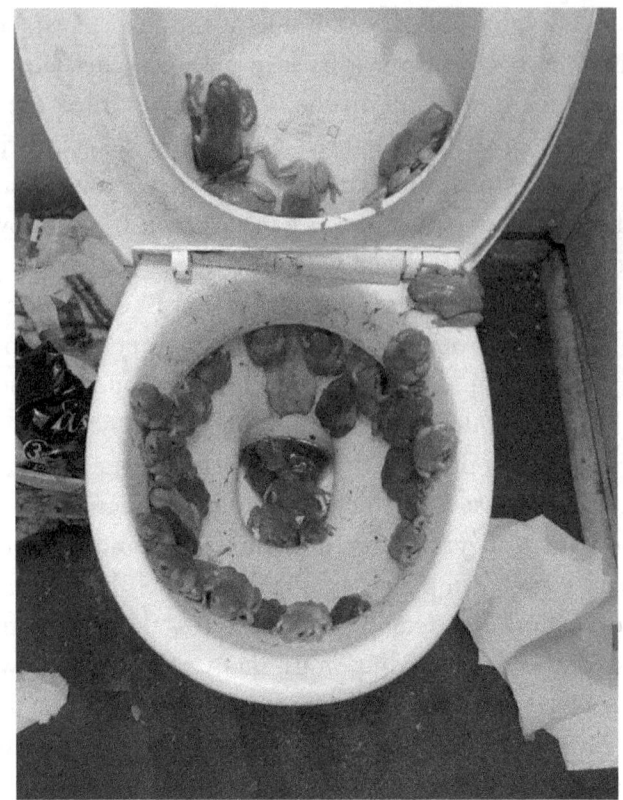

A healthy hatch of toilet toads - they were frogs, actually.

Termite mounds were numerous - some over ten feet high.

We filled the fuel tanks and headed for the deep bush in search of wild Asiatic buffalo, *Bubalus bubalis*. Bob Penfold told me that the local buffalo are the world's largest members of the bovine family which includes American and European bison, African cape buffalo, several species of wild cattle such as Banteng and Gaur, and yaks. These beasts grow to an impressive twelve feet from nose to tail, stand up to six feet tall at the top of the shoulder, weigh up to 2,650 pounds, and can live as long as twenty-five years, and he reminded me that they are at least as hard to kill and as dangerous as the African Cape Buffalo. They are a formidable game, to say the least. These beasts have a "don't mess with me" appearance, similar to that of the African Cape buffalo.

A dense stand of Meleleucca, or gum trees.

In the more open areas, termite mounds towered up to over ten feet above the ground. We pushed one termite tower over with the front bumper, exposing myriads of pale wiggling insects that were immediately set upon by birds. When a Monitor lizard - a Goanna in Aussie lingo - rushed in to join in the feast, the birds set up a cacophony of protesting calls, but kept their distance.

The country here was a mixed woodland with Melaleuca trees (gum trees) and various types of smaller brush interrupting the grassy areas. As we cruised through the trackless bush Bob frequently shut off the engine to listen. For me, the many bird and animal sounds were unfamiliar but delightful.

We heard noises in the distance - men's angry voices. Bob drove toward the tumultuous commotion. Salvos of swear words came exploding our way as we approached their source. Upfront, I saw a large, ancient panel truck and a cut-down Land Cruiser with added steel plates on the sides and attached old tires being used as soft bumpers. It was parked near the edge of a Melaleuca tree to which a large brindle-colored cattle bull was tied. This was the catcher car. Two men were maneuvering the large feral cattle bull, this one - a surly looking part Brahma, that was attached to a tree by a large single rope around its neck. The half-ton beast was struggling and bellowing, throwing its head and blowing long strings of snot in all directions as it lunged back and forth.

We had run across some of the stockman Harower's bull catchers at work.

Scrub bull temporarily tied to a tree.

Immediately I noticed that both bull catchers were barefooted, oblivious to the thorns, sticks, and rocks that littered the ground they trod upon. As the huge wild cattle bull lunged toward one of the men, the other tossed a rope on the ground with the loop wide open in the area where the animal's hind feet would be. Then the teaser man would move to draw the bull toward the loop. After many attempts and resettings of the loop over more than half an hour, the bull finally stepped into the loop and the rope man pulled it tight on one of the critter's hind feet. Holding the rope taunt, he tied it to the bumper of the Toyota and then backed away. This stretched the bull out and partially immobilized the animal.

Quickly the other man walked up to the massive bull, grabbed the tail, and jerked it over. As soon as the body of the animal hit the ground, the man bent the tail in clockwise fashion. Once the tail was bent and held, the bull was unable to regain its feet. Avoiding the remaining three kicking feet and thrashing beast, the two men eventually got both hind feet tied together.

An old panel truck was moved up and was parked nearby the still bellowing, but tired and trussed bull. A heavy rope was run through a pulley in the bed of the truck, out a one-way door (like a pet door), and tied to the rope on the head of the bull. The free end of the pulley rope was then secured to the bumper of the Toyota. As the Toyota backed up, the bawling, struggling bull was drawn up an inclined ramp, through the door and into the big truck. Just before the hind feet went through the door, the rope securing them was released. The captured bull immediately got to its feet and began ramming the rickety sides of its new enclosure. One of the men climbed up on the rack and released the neck rope. The bull was ready to be transported to the station's holding pens. It was soon destined for the slaughterhouse to become ground beef.

This was a good-sized Bubalus bull with medium horns.

The bullcatchers said they had another animal they'd caught that morning tied to a tree and planned to load it next, so we followed them.

The Brahma had put up a good, long fight, but this Bubalus was larger, heavier, much more robust, and it fought a lot harder. The same procedure was followed, but the catcher's car was parked close to the tree to limit the animal's movements and minimize the likelihood of the neck rope breaking. Bob told me that several men had been killed by bulls that broke free of the rope. At one point the bull put a horn through one front tire of the Toyota which elicited a string of swear words from the men. Aussies use somewhat different cuss words than we Americans do, but the point comes across clearly. The man was not happy.

But, after close to half an hour of frustrating, sweaty struggle, one foot was looped, the bull was on the ground and its hind feet were tied. This animal had sharp horns, the tips of which were sawed off before loading to prevent it from killing other captured beasts.

As soon as the bull regained its feet in the truck, it attacked the Brahma. I believe it would have killed its victim if the horns had not been blunted.

The tire had been ruined but was replaced with one of the two spares each catcher vehicle carried. Each turn of the lug wrench and pump of the jack brought a blue streak of cursing from the men.

Bob and I continued on with the survey of the area and our search for large trophy-class Bubalus bulls for the incoming hunters to collect. In all, we counted over forty water buffalo including several impressive males, but Bob told me that he was confident that we could find much better .... meaning larger bulls to shoot as trophies.

Bob's friend, stockman Harrower's, hunting area contained over three million acres, so we had a vast territory to hunt. With both of us intent on seeing as much as possible, using our binoculars and traveling through the more open areas to provide us with the best visibility, seldom did we not have some species of game in the field of view. Kangaroos, Wallabies, Dingos, feral pigs, and smaller animals constantly vied for our attention. In some areas, we found feral donkeys and horses. Feral Dromedary camels imported decades ago from Saudi Arabia inhabited some areas, but we found none that day.

Four days before I had been in Kotzebue, Alaska, thirty-seven miles above the Arctic Circle, now I was in tropical Australia. Ah, the wonders of modern travel.

As we turned back toward the station, we encountered a group of sixteen Bubalus cows and calves accompanied by one large bull lying in a swamp. This bull was a taker and with a full schedule of clients due to arrive the next day, Bob suggested that I attempt to shoot it.

He parked the Land Cruiser, tested the wind, and we began our careful stalk. We had less than a quarter of a mile to walk. As we sneaked along, I saw a relatively nondescript snake less than ten yards away from us and whispered to Bob, but he ignored my message. Later he suggested it might have been a Brown snake, one of the more dangerous neurotoxic serpents in Australia. All snakes are best left alone, or killed, he reminded me.

Using the available cover we closed the range to about thirty-five yards. I took unhurried aim, held for low and just behind the left front shoulder, planning a heart shot, and squeezed the trigger of Bob's .340 Weatherby. At the 250-grain bullet's impact, the bull reared up, raising his front legs, then turned as it came down to look at us. The group of cows and calves bomb-shelled, scattering in all directions, but they only moved about twenty yards before they stopped to look back our way.

"You hit him good, give him another one, mate!" said my friend.

I stuffed another round up the spout, held for the center of the chest, and squeezed again. This time the bull dropped his head a foot or so, then jerked it back up and came a couple of steps our way. This huge beast had the spirit of a devil or a wolverine. The cows and calves ran off to our left, then reassembled about one hundred yards away. They stood watching us.

There was no need to tell me to shoot him again. I placed another in the center of the chest, causing the bull to stagger, then turn to his left, exposing the right shoulder, which I hit with shot number four.

The big bull turned away from us and I placed my fifth shot just under the base of the tail, which dropped the animal straight down on all four legs in the muddy swamp.

The rest of the buffalo mob charged away, leaving a large brown dust trail in their wake.

Yes, *Bubalus bubalis* are tough animals. I shot a very good Cape Buffalo (*Syncerus caffer caffer*) in Rhodesia/Zimbabwe in 1982 that took less pounding to put down. Each of my five shots was sufficient to kill this animal.

The shooting was not at all difficult, nor was the stalk, but the overall experience was indelibly etched in my memory.

As I stood scrutinizing my quarry, Bob trotted back for the vehicle. The daylight was soon to end and we now needed to hustle a bit. I was thinking of the snake I'd seen and possibly other vipers in the vicinity, which I expected to be more active at night.

Upon Bob's arrival a few minutes later, I put the cable on the bull's head and Bob winched it clear of the mud and water to a patch of grass that had been flattened by the resting herd of bovines. We maneuvered the carcass to a position similar to which it had fallen and took some photographs.

I rarely have had shoulder mounts done on the wild game I've taken, so with no need for the cape, removing the head was quickly done. Of course, the neck skin was thick and tough as one might expect. It was not so thick as that of a Pacific Walrus, but thicker than an Alaskan moose, and tough, nevertheless.

I cut out the back straps, tenderloins and heart, leaving the rest of the meat for recovery the following day.

We motored back to the cattle station in the dark, passing many sets of eyes glaring in the headlights.

We enjoyed a quick shower to remove our daily, dusty "Darwin sun tan", then a hearty supper of salad, leg of lamb, and vegetables, followed by freshly baked apple crisp.

What a day this had been! My mind was full of images and impressions from events of the past twelve hours. I would re-live them as I nodded off to sleep and many times more in future years.

Jake and his Bubalus babulis

Bob, Jake and the bull.

On Saturday, July 6, I awoke at 5:00 am, feeling fresh and ready for the new day. Soon the more than thirty little green frogs were chirping in the toilet tank. They were as effective as a rooster crowing at a new dawn. I wondered how they survived. There must be enough insects getting in under the lid to keep them healthy, I figured. I avoided using that toilet as I did not want to flush the cheerful little green buggers into a cesspool.

After breakfast, I skinned the buffalo head and began boiling it in a fifty-five-gallon barrel outside. The hardwood fire quickly brought the water to a rolling boil on this warm windless morning. I added some sal soda to facilitate the removal of muscle attachments. By noon I had cut and scraped off most of the meat, removed the brains, opened the sinuses with a chisel, and completed one re-boil, as Bob readied the camp and gear for the incoming hunters.

After our noon lunch of meat pies, Bob and I drove out to a different area to scout. We sighted buffalo everywhere we went, along with the occasional Dingo and kangaroo. About mid-afternoon, we decided to walk awhile in a more forested area. After a couple of miles of walking, I saw a large striped snake slithering away from us. I thought it might be a Tiger snake, but at about ten feet in length and thick in body, it seemed too large for that species. It did not seem aggressive. I approached the reptile and grabbed it by the end of its tail. The snake rolled back toward me, but I pulled on the tail to keep it off balance. In a few minutes, using a long stick to pin the head, I held it securely behind the head and asked Bob what kind of snake it was.

"There are only two kinds of snakes, mate. Good snakes and bad snakes. That one is alive so it is a bad snake. Now, be careful, but go ahead and make it a good snake", he said.

This snake had a large triangular-shaped head with a black nose but seemed docile. When it began to wrap itself around my arm, I knew it was a constrictor, not a venomous viper, nevertheless, I did not turn loose of its head (it obviously had teeth and I had been painfully bitten by constrictors before). I gently released the serpent, and it hurried on its way.

OFF SEASON PURSUITS

The Carpet Python

Prior to my trip here I had boned up on snakes. As I teenager, with my favorite biology teacher "Catfish McClure" I had caught rattlesnakes, coral snakes, gopher snakes, and Gila Monsters in Arizona which we sold to a dealer in Tucson. I read that Australia has more types of deadly venomous snakes than anywhere else in the world - many of which have neurotoxic venom which results in paralysis and sudden death by asphyxiation.

Then, they've got the Sydney Funnel Web Spider (*Atrax robustus*) - another dangerous inhabitant - but fortunately they are not common on the Top End. Before arriving Down Unda I resolved to be cautious and ever-watchful regarding snakes and insects in this new country. But I had caught a lot of snakes as a teenager and as they say, old habits are hard to break.

The powdery ground held plenty of tracks of cattle, buffalo, and other animals. It was a marvelous, productive game country - and all new to me!

I enjoyed the chewy buffalo back strap with bread and gravy for supper.

Sunday, July 7, after breakfast I cleaned up the sleeping quarters, worked the horns loose from the buffalo skull, did some more cleaning of the skull, and then I set about studying local topographical maps.

Shortly after 1:00 pm a Bonanza single-engine aircraft brought in three German hunters, one wife, and a ten-year-old boy. Bob and I took them out with two Toyotas. After traveling only a few miles from the station we saw about forty buffalo, several Dingos, and a few Kangaroos. One large buffalo bull was taken by Josef, along with a Dingo and a Kangaroo. As is usual for hunters of that culture, the Germans shot well. However, the Toyotas were overheating badly.

Monday, July 8, I awoke early as mosquitos had pestered me all night. I was glad I had long since started my quinidine as a prescribed anti-malarial precaution. Bob flew with the new hunters to hunt feral goats on an island in the Arafura Sea just off the northern tip of Australia. I fired up the kettle for a quick re-boil of my buffalo and skinned Josef's bull before putting it in the kettle water to cook.

Stockman John Harrower stopped by to visit. He asked if I would produce a video for him on his overall operation. That project would require a day in the four-cylinder, 140hp Robertson helicopter and another day in the open vehicles with the bullcatchers. I told him that I would be happy to do so if Bob's operation was not compromised by my absence.

When I inquired about the size of his place, John told me that his cattle station contained about 2,200 square miles, and held an estimated fifteen to twenty thousand cattle and five to eight thousand buffalo. During "the wet" which takes place between December and March, the area is inundated with about forty-four inches of rain - or more!

I drove out to collect wood for the fire and saw a Dingo that was feeding on my buff's gut pile, and shot the wild dog. The stockman wanted all dingos to be shot. This male dingo weighed about fifty pounds. His teeth were all secondary, in perfect condition, but showing little wear, so I assumed it to be a young adult.

Dingoes, *Canis lupus dingo*, that I encountered all looked about the same to me. They are handsome, well-groomed, short-haired canines classified as one of the many subspecies of the grey wolf. Everyone I saw was sandy to reddish brown in color with lighter hues on the chest, belly, and feet. I sighted only solitary dingoes while in Australia.

Off Season Pursuits

A mature Dingo in fine shape.

By 4:00pm Bob returned with the German hunters from the goat hunt. They had three large billies and they'd taken six large feral pigs.

We enjoyed a hearty meal, followed by libations, by all but Penfold. He didn't drink but he kept good supplies for his guests. I was in bed before midnight.

Tuesday, July 9 I boarded the single-passenger helicopter and flew to the Flying Fox River where we hazed wild cattle and buffalo bulls out of the thick bush to areas where the catcher vehicles could maneuver.

The pilot's handling of his chopper was impressive. We were up and down in the woodland, often within a yard of tree tops, sometimes within a few feet of the ground when the animals were standing underneath trees or in swampy areas. The chopper had a loudspeaker device that emitted squeals, whistles, and other alarming noises - all the bells and whistles - to get the bovines to move out of their inaccessible refuges. The downdrafts from the rotors produced billows of dust and debris which often obscured our vision and concealed the movements of the quarry. But, invariably the combination of noise and air disturbance got the bulls moving.

Later I commented to Harrower on the skill of his chopper pilot.

"Yeah, he's good all right, but my former pilot was better until he caught the top of a tree with his rotor blades and killed himself," John told me.

Two catcher vehicles were stripped down Toyota diesel Land Cruisers from which the body had been cut away, leaving only the seats. There were no windshields. Heavy steel plates had been added to the sides. Old tires were attached to the front bumper to cushion the impact with animals, trees, or whatever else they might contact. They were strictly bare-bones machines, but tough enough for the violent work ahead.

A controlled burn was going on, so large sectors of wildland were on fire and some sections had so much smoke we could not work them. The trees seemed to be impervious to the fire, only the grass and low brush burned. We felt thermal updrafts from the fires as we approached.

Bull catching is fast, dusty work. Look at that powdery dust!

When a bull entered an area where they could operate, the catcher cars drove straight at the animal. Initially, most of the bulls attempted to run away, but after being rammed in the butt by the car a few times, most would stand and fight, lowering their heads and charging the tires festooned from the front bumper of each vehicle. Sometimes the catcher cars would get on either side of a running bull to control its direction of travel, but most often a single car would pursue the beast until either it was knocked down, or once the animal was sufficiently tired, a man would jump out, run up behind the beast, get hold of the tail and jerk it to the ground. These bulls were angry and full of fight, so often before he could jerk it off its feet, the man holding the tail had to hang on to avoid being gored. It was the old game of "crack the whip" ... in spades.

It was a pretty hairy business, this bull-catching!

We landed at noon for lunch and a second refueling of the chopper. I was thoroughly enjoying the wild ride, but I had plenty of helicopter footage for Harrower's video, so I joined the bullcatchers in one of the cars for the afternoon.

The bull catchers were paid on a per-head basis and traveled from one cattle station to the next, doing what they did best. This team of catchers was of Aboriginal ancestry and the entire lot were very active, hard-working people. The senior catcher had his wife and kids, the youngest of which was about three years old, - all in the back of his vehicle, while his nephew drove the other vehicle. He told me that they expect to catch and load about twenty bulls per day.

Bull catcher family in their specially rigged vehicle

Well, the chopper activity was of great interest to me and wonderful excitement, but riding in the catcher car was even more gripping.

The catchers would follow along behind the chopper, then hold in a more open area close to the chopper's noisy action. Upon sighting cattle coming into the accessible terrain the cars each picked a bull, herded it away from the dense cover, and began to harass it by bumping it as it attempted to escape. Every bull we pursued that day charged and attempted to gore the catcher's car. Some did so before being bumped, others endured several thumps before turning to fight. Happily, none of the bulls we engaged tried to jump over the outside bumper or get into the vehicle.

As it is with dogs and men, some of the smaller bulls had more fight in them than the larger beasts, but all did put up an admirable struggle.

OFF SEASON PURSUITS

Close quarters in timbered area.
Note the termite mound in the left foreground.

Jerking a scrawny scrub bull down by the tail.

About mid-afternoon a huge *Bubalus* presented in open grassland. The two catcher cars went for it and soon were on either side of the beast as it lumbered along. This animal had a wide sweep of horns, but, lucky for us, it ran straight ahead, never swinging its potentially deadly headgear. After less than a mile of such pursuit, the bull made a slight turn into the front of the catcher car I was filming from and it was knocked to the ground. The momentum of the car thrust it up on top of the huge animal, where it came to a stop. The wheels on the right side of the vehicle were elevated more than a foot above ground level. We were high centered on well over a ton of angry animal, which voiced it's displeasure in loud bellows and kicked as it attempted to regain its footing. As it exhaled, clouds of dust came forth, reminding one of the breaths of a dragon. The critter was pinned. I felt bad for the beast, as I had for trapped Wolverine.

A cattle truck and trailer came to the scene.

The men soon had a large rope on one hind foot which was tied to the other catcher's car. Then the sweaty job of getting the vehicle off of the bull began. Two high lift jacks were used to lift the car, but the bull's thrashing, which intensified when it felt less weight bearing down on it, caused the jacks to slip off, repeatedly. The strength and determination of the great bull were truly impressive. No less so was the determination of the catchers. After nearly a full hour, the bull was freed of its mechanical parasite and dragged a few feet away by the rope. One man held its tail tightly curled toward its nose preventing the bull from regaining its feet.

A large diameter rope was placed around the base of the horns and the bull was stretched out. One of the catchers quickly sawed about four inches off the tip of each horn and the water buffalo was dragged into the big holding trailer. I felt a bit sorry to see such a proud, powerful animal meet its end in that manner. The horns of this bull were the most impressive I had seen.

Buffalo wranglers.

I climbed up on the ramschakle pipe and wooden rack of the trailer to film the operation from above.

Before the big *Bubalus* could get to its feet, a smaller bull began to gore it. This bull had its horns sawn off too, or it, no doubt, would have killed the larger one. Once the bigger bull was standing, it launched into a full-scale head-butting brawl with the other buffalo and a cattle bull that I'm sure was wishing he was somewhere else. The goring thrusts rocked the trailer and I reminded myself that if I fell into the trailer, I would quickly meet my Maker. It took several minutes for the enraged animals to settle down, but loud angry bellows continued to punctuate the scene every few seconds. None seemed to like the company it had suddenly been thrust into.

The tally for this day was ten wild cattle bulls, the large *Bubalus,* and one smaller buffalo bull - a bit less than an average daily total, I was told.

The captured animals were not happy, bellowing and roaring constantly.

Stockman John Harrower told me that twenty years ago, and without the use of a helicopter, he was catching up to fifty bulls per day.

I remembered seeing a film of Aussies catching wild buffalo similar to the experience I had just enjoyed, but they used a mechanical arm to reach out and clamp the beast behind the head. I did not see a machine like that on Harrower's cattle station.

A new "bionic arm" bull-catching machine.

Later in the year the round-up or muster would take place. For that, John and his blokes, instead of going barefooted, wore boots, to which they could attach spurs because some of the horses were a bit salty, he said.

Wednesday, July 10 began with a dry wind, but clear skies. Josef shot his second buffalo, then the rush was on to meet the incoming plane and new hunters. We drove to the Flying Fox River where two of the three hunters took the two largest buffalo of the year, each measuring over one hundred inches in scoring points. We had not seen these bulls prior to today. Apparently, they had come off the nearby escarpment. I wondered how many more monstrous *Bubalus* might be nearby.

A very good Bubalus

Just before sundown, one of Harrower's "blokes" drove me around to show the domestic stock. He had some of the largest and finest-looking Brahma cattle I've ever seen. He also had two albino *Bubalus* in one paddock.

Thursday, July 11, It was a bit chilly last night and I slept very well. Just after a quick breakfast, we departed at 7:30 am for South Goulburn Island for goats. We deplaned and went directly to the beach where Bob swam out to an open boat anchored thirty yards offshore. As he swam out, I was wondering about saltwater crocodiles which are known to inhabit the area.

Thirty minutes of boat travel took us to North Goulburn Island. Bands of goats were everywhere. The hunters had a marvelous selection of old billies and each shot at least one. I did not care to take a feral goat, so after filming the others I went back to the beach where I had seen numerous Nautilus shells that had washed up. I collected nine of the beautiful shells.

We retraced our morning travel and returned to Mountain Valley just at dark. After supper, I washed some of my clothes and watched my "Darwin suntan" go down the shower drain.

A good Golburn Island Billy

Beautiful Nautilus shells littered the beaches.

Friday, July 12, Bob flew off to the Dorisvale tent camp while I took a hunter out for another buffalo. After about two hours we found a good bull among a herd of nineteen. These animals had been spooked by our noisy motorized approach and charged away. We followed on foot and within a half hour found a shooting opportunity at about sixty yards.

I cautioned the hunter to take his time and be sure of his shot. He was using a .458 and was confident. I, too, was confident as previously I had seen him shoot very well. I got ready with the video camera. At the bullet's impacting the right shoulder, the bull dropped to his knees, keeping his hindquarters in the air. As the bull struggled to get up I told the hunter to smack him again. The second heavy bullet found its mark just behind the right front shoulder and rolled the bull.

We approached the downed giant from his blind side, but he sensed our presence and tried to raise his head, so at a range of twenty yards, I had the hunter put another 400-grain round into the base of the neck. After the third shot, the buffalo's only movement was that of its blood spurting onto the dry grass.

During this shooting I was able to video the entire sequence for use in the promotional film for Hunt Australia, with my borrowed .340 Weatherby slung on my shoulder. I'm convinced that the .340 is the "killingest" caliber.

By mid-afternoon, we were back at the cattle station and Bob came in with the aircraft to transport us to Dorisvale.

A negative mood seemed to mute the usual vocal camp exhilaration. One of the new hunters, a non-revenue "freebie" guest, was complaining about trivial things. As they say, "no good deed goes unpunished" and in my experience, the "freebies" are most often the source of irrelevant, picayune protests in hunting camps.

Bob's wife, Kay, was noticeably upset, so I offered to help with dishes, bedding and general chores.

"What do you think Bob talks about most often when he's away on booking trips," I asked Kay as we were cleaning up the dining area.

"Me, I reckon," she replied.

"Righto" was my reply.

She laughed and the atmosphere seemed to improve. In busy times, insignificant stuff too often gets in the way of one's appreciation of what is really important.

Saturday, July 13 marked the beginning of my second week "down unda." The temperature had cooled off some, which made our walking hunt for pigs very pleasant. We covered six or seven kilometers, sighting a dozen or more black hogs, but none were shot. The "freebie" guest and one other hunter in my group saw pigs, but did not shoot as the swine spooked and never did stop to offer an easy shot. Many hunters, especially Europeans, simply will not shoot at a running animal. Soon the complainer again had the entire camp in a negative mood. I suggested that tame or penned pigs might offer easier shots for him, but no one commented on that.

The next morning a charter plane arrived and made two trips to Darwin with the departing guests. Bob and I drove the two Toyotas to Darwin after the second plane departed. I enjoyed a wonderful time in this outback country of Australia's "Top End" and was not looking forward to leaving. My memories of the chirping green toilet toads - or frogs, the large flocks of Galahs that visited the cattle station each morning, and the overall abundance of game, the entire experience made me feel like I should stay longer ... or return as soon as possible. But I kept reminding myself that my main interest had been focused on the Rusa deer which we planned to soon be hunting.

Monday morning, July 15, Bob was able to get an appointment with a chiropractor in Darwin. His back had been bedeviling him for the past two weeks. He seemed somewhat improved when we boarded the jet at 1:00 pm. After a brief stop in Brisbane, we arrived in Sidney at 7:30 pm, got a quick bite to eat, and drove on to his home in Newcastle, arriving just after midnight.

Penfold's phone and fax machine were busy all night it seemed. I awoke numerous times due to the ringing. Early the next morning we drove to the downtown area for Bob to see another chiropractor. I looked around the smaller shops and found some nice opals, still in the mother rock, so I bought several pendants to take home. Bob's youngest daughter, Julie, made a wonderful supper of lamb, potatoes, salad, and a dessert. I went to bed feeling satisfactorily stuffed and looking forward to the next stop

NEW CALEDONIA

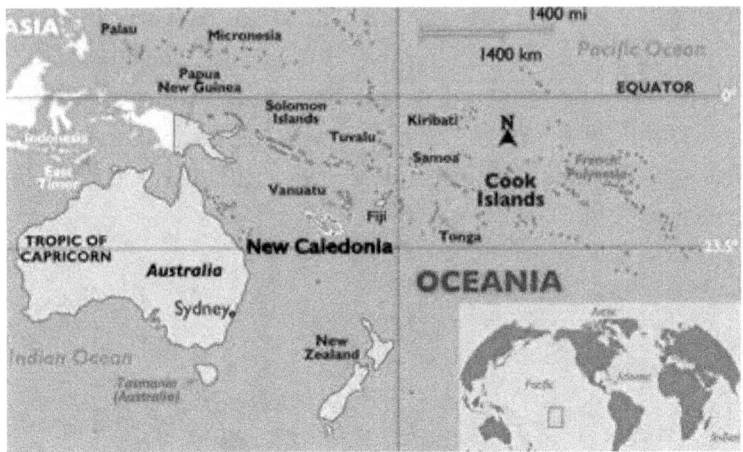

New Caledonia lies 1,490km east of
Australia and 628km southeast of Vanuatu.

Wednesday, July 17 we were up at 4:30 am for the drive to Sidney International Airport. Initially, there was some confusion regarding my need for a Visa for entry to New Caledonia. After some heated discussions between ticket agents and government officials, the consensus was that no Visa was required for U.S. citizens. But they were divided in their opinion. Well, if I was turned back at Noumea, I figured I'd just have to return to Sidney. If no Visa was requested, or demanded, I would not bring up the issue.

The jet made a short stop in Brisbane, then took us to Noumea, the capital of New Caledonia. During the flight, I reviewed my notes on the area.

The group of islands called New Caledonia is officially a "collectivity" of France. (Read that colony.) People of French ancestry outnumber those of the Kanak culture, the original, native inhabitants of the area.

Captain James Cook gave the area its name as it reminded him of Scotland. Initially, the harvest of sandalwood drew Europeans to the area. When that trade declined, "Blackbirding" - the term for the enslavement of natives for work in the sugar cane plantations of Fiji and Queensland - was the principal attraction.

Cannibalism was historically practiced as part of the Kanak culture. But I did not find any recipes for their "long pig" dishes. I doubted it would be on the official menu, but I did scrutinize the menu listings in the restaurant.

The United States established the headquarters for the Navy and Army in the South Pacific in Noumea in 1942. It was during that U.S. presence that wild turkeys from the United States were introduced to New Caledonia.

The discovery of nickel in 1864 sparked French mining efforts and generated some world interest in New Caledonia. International demand led to "the nickel boom" of 1969 to 1972. Agitation for political power by the native Kanaks in 1988 led to hostage taking and several deaths of Kanaks and one policeman when French commandos assaulted the Kanak stronghold on one of the eastern islands. All of the hostages survived the experience. Periods of tension between the European and native residents have checkered the political scene in New Caledonia for the past several decades. Importation of firearms and ammunition restrictions had varied from year to year.

Then I reviewed what I had found on Javan Rusa deer (*Cervus timorensis*). Native only to Java and Bali, this species has been introduced to Australia and many islands of the Indo-Pacific region. These deer are able swimmers and have extended their range to adjacent islands throughout the area. The Javan Rusa are known to hybridize with the much larger Sambar deer. That would make an interesting critter! Rusa deer seem to prefer some types of grasses but include herbs, leaves, and the bark of shrubs and seaweed in their diet. So they both graze and browse. Rusa tend to remain segregated by sex, except during the time of the rut, the peak of which is in mid-July in New Caledonia. We were arriving at prime time for Rusa hunting.

Rusa stags stand a shade under four feet tall at the shoulder, weigh up to 255 pounds, and normally have unbranched antlers with three tines on each side. The females (hinds) are about twenty to thirty percent smaller and do not have antlers. So, I would be expecting the size of the deer to be similar - perhaps a tad heavier - to that of the Sitka Blacktail deer, which populate the Kodiak Archipelago. Penfold assured me that New Caledonia had the largest Rusa deer in the world.

The jet took us North East of Australia to New Caledonia which is an archipelago about 750 miles from Brisbane. The largest island, Grande Terre, is an elongated tropical land mass of about 7,000 square miles, running North West to South East approximately 320 miles in length and about forty to sixty miles in width.

We landed at Noumea, a city with a human population of about 90,000, without incident. The customs people inspected my Passport and made no mention of a Visa. I sighed in relief.

We were delayed over two hours getting a previously reserved rental van - such governmental inefficiency to be expected in remote French-controlled areas, as I came to realize. Then we drove on to purchase some groceries. I was surprised to see the prices were on par with the extortionate fees charged for goods in rural Alaska.

From the airport at Noumea Bob and I drove on a good road about 115 miles north to Bourail, which is about midway up the west side of the big island, arriving about 1:30 am and feeling fatigued. This pleasant little town had about 4,800 residents, who for the most part had well-kept houses and shops. Bourail means lizard tail in one of the local dialects. We motored on a few more miles to a cattle station called Guaro Diva, where we stretched out in the back of the van, and turned in for the night.

The morning of July 18 was clear and calm. A fresh Rusa stag skull with thirty-inch antlers - trophy quality - was hanging on the fence. The cattle station owner told us that he estimated eight to ten thousand Rusa were on his acreage and he preferred that the number be reduced.

A seventeen-kilometer road led to an old bat cannery that Penfold had leased to serve as his hunting headquarters. We transferred our gear to a rented Land Rover and set off. Immediately we began seeing Rusa deer. Many stags were roaring and their blood - and ours - was up. It sounded like the hills were full of roaring lions. About three miles shy of the cannery we had a flat tire. The spare was in good shape, but no lug wrench was in the vehicle (those bloody French !), so we walked the remaining distance, up and down the hills, in slick mud. At the cannery, we located a crescent wrench large enough to engage the lugs. Then we slogged back to change the tire.

After stowing our gear in the spacious building we drove back to Bourail for more food and other supplies, the acquisition of which was complicated and inevitably delayed by the French lingo, attitude, and protocol. We went to a restaurant for a nice dinner of "whiskey shrimp." Within thirty minutes I broke out in hives - itchy lumps on my head, neck, chest and back, but they quickly subsided. Nevertheless, I resolved to never eat eat shrimp again - and for the last 36 years I have not tasted shrimp. We retired early. Bob's aching back was giving him a hard time.

Friday, July 19 we secured two .243 rifles for the guest hunters to use. We endured more hassles getting supplies. It seems the French must always complicate simple issues. We returned to Guaro Diva and drove on to the bat cannery. I remained at the cannery to repair the windmill and shoot some fresh meat as Bob went back to Noumea to pick up some guest hunters, along with his cook and her husband. He said he would return late in the afternoon of the following day.

The windmill fix was quick and easy, requiring only the reattachment of a brace and tightening a few nuts, so I took one of the rifles, fired it at a target only once, which was satisfactory, and walked up over the nearest hill.

Wild turkeys, *Meleagris gallopavo*, which looked to me just like the ones I had hunted in Arizona and New Mexico (Merriam's or Gould's turkeys) , were everywhere and in all stages of development. Some hens were on their nests, gobblers were strutting and fighting ... it was the best turkey hunting I had ever seen. It was absolutely wonderful!

Walking up the hill behind the cannery I encountered several flocks of the big birds. One of the bunches was composed entirely of large gobblers. It was not difficult to get to within thirty yards of the group and when one bearded fellow uphill from me stood clear of the others, I held just beneath the head and squeezed. The turkey hit the ground and began to rapidly flap its wings, giving rise to a mini dust devil and the panicked departure of its companions. The rented rifle was accurate. Turkey hunting had never before been so easy for me.

New Caledonia's turkeys were introduced from the USA during WWII.

Hearing a deep-throated stag roaring in the valley below, I set off with the turkey tied to my pack board, to locate the source of the noise. As I coursed through the broken woodland I found Rusa deer everywhere. Several times hinds (females) saw me, looked straight at me, and stamped their front feet, before turning and running away. I could distinguish at least a dozen different stags roaring from all quadrants.

Upon reaching the valley floor I startled two feral pigs, whose explosive exit from a nearby bush startled me. Those black hogs appeared to be of about sixty to seventy pounds in weight and disappeared into the thick bush near a small stream that flowed toward the ocean. I planned to eat wild pork soon.

The stag that had originally attracted me seemed to be coursing around in one thick patch of timber and brush. After an hour and a half of cautious stalking, I was convinced that this animal's roars were the lowest octave of all that I had heard. I assumed that this indicated a larger, older animal. But I was catching only glimpses of the dark form of the deer as he moved busily about, occasionally thrashing a bush, chasing off smaller stags, and riding herd on his harem of hinds. With only fleeting views of the antlers, I was not certain that I was seeing the best stag in the area or that he was even a taker. With so many other animals on the move in the dense limber and brush, I was concerned that one animal might detect my presence, stomp and snort an alarm, and take the whole bunch away in a rush, so I crept along very slowly.

When from a twisted position, bent around a tree, I glassed him at seventy yards, he had just risen from a mud wallow, shook his head, and stood still. He was unaware of my presence. I froze in place in that uncomfortable posture, but I could finally evaluate his headgear. This fine stag had at least thirty-inch main beams with brow points and mid-beam points of about nine or ten inches on each antler. I counted four hinds and one smaller stag in close proximity to the dominant deer. But I was sure there were more nearby in the dense brush. Some might be larger.

Normally I would defer taking a good trophy so early in the hunt, especially if the beast was of a species with which I was unfamiliar, but we did need some fresh meat, the country was new to me and the afternoon was waning. Bob had mentioned that if time allowed I might take more than one stag. So I shot it in the neck, just behind the head. The stag collapsed straight down on its belly. The other deer scattered immediately, making a chirping noise as they fled.

This Rusa had 32 inch antlers.

I was pleased with this fine stag, but if circumstances permitted, after helping the guest hunters take their trophies and becoming more familiar with the species, I might get a chance to select an even better one.

In all, I saw over sixty Rusa that afternoon. I fired two shots at wild game, had two good animals, and kept the spent cases for surrender to the police at the end of the trip. That made it a very good day.

After quartering the Rusa, boning out the neck, back straps, and tenderloins, chopping lose the ribs, and loading it on my pack board, I needed to hurry to get to the top of the ridge and orient myself for the return to the cannery. The country was a dense jungle interspersed with grasslands, but I was new here and wanted to be sure of my return route. I was told there were no poisonous snakes or spiders on this island.

I had departed with only a small coil of nylon parachute cord, my knife, a small hatchet, matches, a small flashlight, and a quart of water in the little sack on my pack frame. The meat of the deer weighed about sixty pounds. I tied the four legs together and carried the load over my shoulder. I slung the rifle and carried the head - another eighteen pounds - in one hand and the unplucked turkey - about sixteen pounds - in my other hand. By staying clear of the dense thickets when possible, the going was not difficult, so my load was quite manageable. But I missed my Alaska packboard.

There were lots of huge, colorfully marked spiders with freshly spun webs in the forest areas. I tried to avoid the arachnids, but as the light dimmed, I got into their pestiferous webs several times. The big spiders did not act aggressively, to my relief. Those large bugs were the only negative thing I found that afternoon.

It was just past sunset when I sighted the clearing that held the cannery. There was a relatively open, downhill route and I took my time, using my flashlight, or torch, as the Aussie blokes call them.

Upon reaching the headquarters I took off my pack, drank two full glasses of cool water, and hung the deer meat in a small shed to keep birds away, before dining on a tin of beef with crackers, tea, some cookies, or sweet biscuits as the blokes Down Unda call them, and a piece of fruit. I plucked and gutted the turkey before hanging it next to the deer meat. Finally, I generously sprinkled coarse ground black pepper on the meat to discourage flies. A small amount of salt spread onto the meat would help it firm up, so I sprinkled some salt on it, too.

After washing up a bit - I'd sweat plenty in the humid tropical conditions - I climbed into my bunk just before midnight. It had been a very fine day. The deep-throated roaring of numerous stags serenaded me to sleep.

Saturday, July 20, I was up at 4:30 am. Stags roaring and hinds chirping were delightful music to my ears, though the local French people we had talked with in Bourail complained about the racket.

The repaired windmill was turning and water was flowing cool and plenty. The hanging meat was cool to the touch and had a firm crust with no sign of flies. It should age and keep well for a few days, even in those warm, moist conditions.

Bob Penfold was due back in the late afternoon with the cook, her husband, and two guest hunters. With stags tuned up and turkeys gobbling, I hastily swept the floors, gobbed out some large spider webs from the rooms, and looked for other chores. Finding nothing I needed to do, I set off to explore a new area. At the edge of the clearing, just 100 yards from the cannery, I jumped a single pig that scooted off into the creek bottom and was gone. The thought of roasting wild pork enticed me, but I resisted pursuing the hog, thinking that another turkey would be adequate, given the number of mouths to be fed that evening. What a hunters' paradise this was!

Figuring that I had about five hours to tromp around, I headed for the highest hills. Deer were everywhere from the riparian areas in the valley floor to the sidehills and the tops of the higher terrane. A large shed antler was lying near a mud hole and I soon located the opposite side nearby. This set had thirty-two-inch main beams and having been sheltered from direct sunlight, they had retained their beautiful dark brown color. I rigged them together to serve as a pack frame. I tied them to my pack board and soon found other sheds, most often only a single side. My hastily fashioned pack board took on the appearance of a load of firewood.

With turkeys so abundant I decided to put off shooting one until I was close to the cannery on my return.

Rusa deer, even in such great numbers, are still deer .... normally alert and twitchy. The Rusa deer in the area we were hunting, Guaro Diva, were as free of contact with mankind as one could expect to find any place in the world, but stalking them required careful, thoughtful technique. Once they sensed the presence of people, they immediately stomped their front feet, chirped and rushed to safety in the thick bush. They seemed to rely heavily on their eyes, but on at least one occasion when a slight zephyr came up behind me and spooked nearby deer, I was sure they had caught my odor.

Many opportunities were presented to observe and film these interesting Cervids that day and with no one else along to add to the possibility of spooking the animals, I took advantage of this unique opportunity. I filmed stags fighting, rolling in their mud wallows, feeding, and resting. I also filmed several stags that had more impressive headgear than the one I shot the day before. Now my primary concern was with getting as much footage on tape as possible in order to put together a good thirty-minute promotional piece for Penfold. This was great fun, but much more demanding than stalking an animal to shoot. Of course, time flies fastest when one is engaged in such an interesting endeavor and all too soon I had to head back to the cannery.

I had left a note on the table indicating where I had gone and that I intended to return by dark or shortly thereafter. Nevertheless, I hustled back in the diminishing daylight. About a mile short of my destination, I found a good bunch of tom turkeys and shot one which was a bit larger than the gobbler of the day before.

The cook, who with her husband, was busy preparing dinner when I came in. She was a pleasant older lady from New Zealand. I told her I would pluck and clean the freshly killed bird at her convenience, probably after the meal.

Bob's guest hunters were named Rich and John. John was the editor of Gunsports magazine. Both men were keyed up for the coming hunt.

Sunday, July 21 we were up and having cereal and coffee at 4:30 am. I realized that I had only one more week before having to board the jet and return to Arctic Alaska, and I wanted to make the most of the remaining days in this tropical paradise. Rick and I struck off to the area I had scouted the day before, while Bob took John up the hill behind the cannery. Stags had been roaring all night and seemed to take no break during the daylight hours. It's impossible for me to not be enthusiastic in such a situation.

Rich was a very thoughtful, careful hunter with a lot of experience chasing deer. He was a great companion, very quiet in the field, and a good walker and observer. We looked at over three hundred deer that day, including a large non-typical stag with four long points on the right antler. It was the only non-typical Rusa I saw. I filmed the odd stag at less than one hundred yards, but Rich wanted to hold out for a typical head. He was a very disciplined fellow who had budgeted trophy fees for one stag only and stuck to it. I probably should have shot that non-typical one myself.

In Alaska, a guide may not take any game while assisting booked clients - which is a good regulation - but no such restriction is applied here. However, I decided to pass up the unique non-typical.

We found three groups of feral pigs and countless turkeys, adding to the wonder of the place for both of us. Every day we found lots of big, colorful spiders, but, spooky as they looked, they were not bothersome.

We noticed the great biodiversity of the plants wherever we walked, both in leafy trees and those with needles. I had never seen most of those species of trees and shrubs anywhere else, nor had I been exposed to some of those exotic fragrances. Rich told me the vegetation was different all right, but not so radically different to him, as many of the plants he had seen in New Zealand. Two years later, on another filming trip for Penfold, I would get the chance to witness the modern "carboniferous forest" of New Zealand's South Island.

Having delicious lunches supplied by the cook and refiling our water containers from the numerous springs, we made a long day of that trip.

Shortly after our lunch, Bob and John appeared on a ridge line a mile south of us, so we joined them. As the four of us walked through a densely forested hillside, Bob held up his hand for all to stop. Not eighty yards from us stood a very impressive stag looking straight our way. Bob motioned for John to come up. I got my camera out and began to film. This great beast appeared to be alone. He gave an occasional roar, moved very little, and kept his eyes on us. After ten minutes, John got a clear shot and he dropped the stag with a bullet to the neck. This stag was all anyone could dream of in a Rusa. His main beams measured over thirty-four inches. His brows and mid-antler points were all taped between ten and twelve inches and were precisely symmetrical. Bob said he would place in the top ten of the Safari Club International record book. This was the first deer that John had ever taken. What a way to start!

John said he would take only that one stag, as it would be hard to beat.

We had an unhurried walk back for supper, returning just before dark to the smells of something wonderful in the oven. It was a roast wild turkey.

Someone, most likely the cook's husband, shot a feral pig weighing about sixty pounds that day, which we saw hanging with the other meat.

Monday, July 22 Bob and I were up at 4:00 am for the drive to Bourail to visit a farmer who had invited Bob to come for a look-see. Before dawn, we walked about his pastures and heard many roaring stags, but they kept out of sight. I took this opportunity to record the wonderful stag music. We took a look at the man's personal trophies which included one huge rack which Bob scored as the largest ever recorded. A large non-typical rack, similar to the one I had seen the day before, with a second main beam on the right side hung beside it. This farmer had dozens of deer racks, most of which were in his barn. He obviously liked to hunt and eat Rusa venison. The entire collection was impressive.

Our breakfast in Bourail consisted of two eggs, bacon, bread, and coffee at ten dollars per plate- a high price for such a meal in 1991! Shopping through the high-priced food and other supplies kept us in town until noon. Price-wise, I felt right at home, as if I were in Hanson's Trading Company, in Kotzebue, Alaska.

Back at the camp, I had the afternoon to myself so I went up another valley to film and scout for exceptional heads I saw scores of stags, picked up six shed antlers, and found the intact skull of a stag with the most massive and heavily pearled antlers I had seen to date. These antlers were bleached out, indicating they had lain in place for some time, probably a couple of years or more. There was no sign of rodents gnawing the bone or antlers. Of course, I packed the head back to the camp, intending to keep it, but the cook wanted it, so I cheerfully gave it to her.

July 23, Tuesday began with light rainfall. Rich, John, and I departed at 8:00 am as the shower diminished, a bit later than usual for the start of our day.. We were hoping to find the stag with the extra point that I had filmed two days earlier, but after thoroughly crisscrossing the area he had occupied, we did not locate it. We set off to locate four deep-throated stags vocalizing in an adjacent area, but the non-typical was not one of them. Again, we saw many trophy-class stags.

The rain brought the humidity to maximum and the muggy conditions had us sweating like chain gang ditch diggers. We drank from springs and streams without a second thought, thankful for the uncontaminated water.

"FLyng foxes" - giant fruit bats.

From an elevated hillside, we noticed what appeared to be large black birds active in one draw across the valley. When we got closer we realized that the birds were actually giant fruit bats, or flying foxes, as they are called. These bats had wing spreads of over four feet and I estimated their body weight to be about three to four pounds - a tad less weighty than an adult Snowshoe hare. Years before I had seen live bats hanging in markets in Thailand, apparently destined for a cooking pot. The local French said the fruit-eating bats were delicious and the cannery we were using had been built for exporting their flesh to European markets. I was interested in sampling one, but my companions told me that I could eat it all by myself, as they were not interested in tasting any of it. With the limited ammunition and total lack of enthusiasm of my friends, I decided not to waste a round on a hanging bat.

We experimented with calling deer, emulating both stags and chirping hinds. It was partially effective. As we walked I found three large shed antlers which I gave to John and Rich.

We were back at the headquarters at 6:45 pm, just in time to dine on freshly roasted wild pork.

New Caledonia

Bob came in with a new hunter from the States.

It rained most of that night, but the morning sky was only partly cloudy. We rose to the alarm at 4:00 am, ate a quick breakfast topped off with fresh scones, grabbed our lunches, and were off. We walked through a saddle in the northern range of hills and met a gusty wind with intermittent showers.

In my experience game is more twitchy in windy conditions, but the Rusa deer seemed to remain in the heavy cover and if anything, were less alert than usual that morning. We found a superb stag and after nearly an hour of maneuvering, Rich shot him in a small forest clearing. To our surprise and pleasure, this stag had a small third antler. It was only a two-inch spike, but that made the trophy so unique. Later that evening Bob scored the head at 120 points.

Rich and his heavy beamed, three antlered stag.

This animal had a decent cape, not so scarred and damaged as most. I caped it for a shoulder mount, tied the meat on my board and we were back at camp by 2:00 pm. In my view, though not the highest scoring, this was the most impressive and attractively formed Rusa rack taken that week. Rich's patience and discrimination had certainly paid off for him.

We'd both muddied ourselves and sweat plenty, so I bathed and washed some clothes before going back out with John and Rich. I got some very nice footage of several stags, intermittently roaring on a skyline at sunset. We were back for dinner at 7:00 pm.

July 25 John, Rich, and I departed at 6:00 am, again to try to locate the non-typical stag. We saw one hundred and eight hinds and fawns, over fifty stags, innumerable turkeys, and two pigs, but did not find the unusual stag. The roaring was constant in the morning, but the hills grew quiet in the afternoon.

Bob and the new hunter returned with a fine stag. We all celebrated over a big dinner of venison, pork, turkey and wine. Bob told me he thought I should spend the next day as I pleased.

July 26 I was up at 4:00 am, swigged a cup of coffee, grabbed my lunch, and struck off down country toward the ocean with rifle and camera. I found plenty of signs and more shed antlers, but fewer deer in the lower country. I continued a bit into the mangrove wetlands where I saw some fish I figured to weigh four to five pounds and decided to head back up the country for deer.

Once again I got some good footage of stags in mud wallows, including one large fellow with, unfortunately, a broken right main beam. I found and filmed more stags fighting, but I could not locate the non-typical one.

Late in the afternoon, I glassed a dandy stag across the valley. This dominant male had his attention divided between a large band of hinds and three other mature males. He was rushing back and forth from harem to chase off one interloper, then another, and back to the females, which would have allowed me an easy stalk if not for there being so many animals between me and the one I wanted. I was concerned that one of the hinds would see me and give an alarm taking the whole bunch away, and it was too late in the day to pursue that stag over the next hill, into another valley, and maybe lose him.

I found a good tree branch for a rest and squeezed the trigger at about 250 yards. It appeared that the bullet struck the big stag a bit low, but just behind the shoulder. The wounded animal charged down the hill into thick brush. The other deer bomb-shelled and were gone.

The heart hangs low on all deer, so I expected he would not go far before bleeding out. It took me only twenty minutes to locate my quarry, lying dead in a tangle of vines and under brush. It had been a heart shot. I was pleased with this battered, scarred old Rusa stag.

I spent forty minutes dragging the stag uphill to an open saddle for a photo.

My stag had 36-inch main beams.

Knowing I was going to be after dark getting back to camp, I hustled with the butchering. The cape of my animal was badly scarred and I prefer just the bleached skull and antlers anyway, so I saved some time on that issue.

As I headed back I found a matched pair of thirty-three-inch sheds, so I carried them back as well.

With the overcast thickening, it was quite dark for the last hour of my trip and I stumbled several times and came in looking like a mud wrestler.

It took me two and a half hours to reach the camp. The rest of the crew were finishing up their dinner. The cook said she had been worried about me.

"I knew you'd be out as long as possible, no worries from me, mate, glad you got such a super stag", Bob assured me.

After wolfing down a big dinner I began boiling the head, with the skin on, which makes it peel away much easier than if the skin is removed prior to boiling. The skull had to be free of blood, meat, and smell to get through customs. I expected extra scrutiny and officiousness from the Frenchmen, so I spent over two hours on that chore.

Penfold had been to Bourail and was told by the local gendarmes that no permits were available. We would have to get the papers in Noumea. That would probably mean untoward bureaucratic delays before checking in for the jet.

We had enjoyed a special week in the undisturbed outback of New Caledonia. Each of Bob's guest hunters had taken a fine trophy Rusa .. and I had, too. I believe this hunt was as enjoyable a deer hunt as any in which I had participated. It is the only deer hunt which I could compare with Sitka Blacktail deer hunting on Kodiak Island.

One could enjoy a very good life in New Caledonia, especially if the governmental intrusive interference was eliminated.

On departure day, July 25 we awoke at five o'clock in the morning, ate a quick breakfast, and sped toward Noumea. Our jet was not scheduled to depart until mid-afternoon, but we were allowing for delays in securing the necessary documents for importation to Australia and for me, to the United States. I had brought along my buffalo from Australia which confused the French customs officials, but that paperwork was intact and properly done, so with scowling misgivings, the gendarmes let it go with me. We spent nearly an hour with each Rusa skull as it was repeatedly inspected and fondled by all three agents before the permits were stamped and approved. Our ammunition plus spent cases tally was right, so we got a pass on that issue.

But the French official said we needed one more piece of paperwork. He brought a stack of forms from a locked drawer and then said those forms could only be issued on Fridays. But we were scheduled to depart that day, which was Thursday.

Four fine Rusa kills and one sun- bleached pick-up rack.

The official placed the forms back in the drawer and closed it, but before he could lock the drawer, Penfold put on a show.

Penfold grabbed his chest and moaned, then, as he staggered, he gasped that he may be having a heart attack and needed help getting to his medicine in the vehicle. As he struggled out the door with the official close behind, Bob winked at me.

I grabbed six or eight copies of the form and put them inside my shirt before following Bob and the Frenchman to his vehicle. Bob nervously opened a small pill container and swallowed one pill. I caught his glance and nodded and winked.

Penfold's chest pain quickly disappeared and his recovery was rapid, so we gathered up our trophies and departed the office before anyone realized I had taken the forms we needed. Though a bit damp from my sweat, they would serve us well. Had I not done that, we would have been forced to stay another week in Noumea.

As we drove toward the airport we passed a Club Med near the beach and close by was a snake, dead on the road. I had been concerned about serpents in the dense bush but was assured that there were no snakes in New Caledonia. Perhaps this was someone's pet serpent that had escaped.

I regretted leaving Noumea and beautiful New Caledonia.

Before the jet departed Noumea I thanked Bob for a wonderful time and he thanked me for the extra forms. The Qantas jet landed three hours later in Sydney. John gave me a lift to a nearby motel and I made the plane for Los Angeles in the morning. I dozed some during the thirteen-hour Boeing 747 flight over the Pacific, but I felt tired when we landed at LAX.

The customs officials had been a pain in Noumea, but the one I first encountered in Los Angeles was the most rude, ignorant, and obstinate person I had ever been forced to deal with in such a situation. My buffalo skull was packaged along with some shed Rusa antlers and the two racks of cleaned and bleached skulls I was bringing home. I had the two Bubalus buffalo horns in my other piece of checked luggage. When the stupid, officious black woman saw them, she blurted out in her version of barely understandable pigeon English that Rhino horns were illegal.

Remaining calm, I told her that indeed, Rhino horns were illegal, but these were buffalo horns. I explained that clearly there was a right and a left horn, whereas Rhinos have a fore and aft horn. Furthermore, Rhino horns are solid structures, without a hollow core, which these horns clearly showed.

The customs woman said she was going to confiscate the Rhino horns. I asked that she contact the supervisor.

"I AM, the supavisah, sir," the affirmative action employee angrily retorted.

Two other inspectors nearby observed the goings on at my table.

"Then call in someone of higher authority and with normal intelligence, as these are clearly not Rhino horns and I have a plane to catch at another terminal very soon," I suggested.

The "supavisah" was very upset. The other two inspectors joined us, handled the horns, and said they did not believe them to be Rhino horns.

"But yo not sure about that, are you," the "supavisa" said, as her increasing decibels attracted attention throughout the large room.

"I do not intend to leave those horns in your hands, but I do expect to file a complaint due to your incompetence and rude demeanor and demand that your boss see to transporting me and my luggage to my check-in gate in time for my flight to Alaska," I told her.

By now the "supavisa" was so angry she could not speak. From across the room, a male official approached us and asked what the problem was. He held each horn up and verified they were not Rhino horns, were properly documented by Australia, and should be allowed to enter the United States.

This confrontational melee had consumed more than a full hour and I told the new man that I had a long way to go to reach my gate. The fellow called in an electric car and helped load my two checked bags on it. I asked for a complaint form, but due to my time constraints, he said he would mail one to me. I gave him my business card which included my mailing address. I had a pleasurable escorted trip through the congested throngs of people to my designated gate. But I never did receive a complaint form. I would have enjoyed seeing that miserable "supervisa" chastised or fired.

The "supavisa" was still shouting in the background as we silently motored away. I told the cart driver that I hoped they would fire her, muzzle her, or give her a broom. He made no comment.

After a short stop in San Francisco, I flew on to Anchorage without further incident. I had spent four weeks in wonderful new territories and was loaded with mental images and memories of this great trip.

Monday, July 29, I gathered up some groceries at a discount store, shipped them to Kotzebue, and boarded the Boeing 727 for Kotzebue. I sat next to my friend, former Governor Jay Hammond, and enjoyed a nice visit with that admirable man.

The next summer Bob and Kay visited us at Kodiak and we enjoyed some superb fishing for halibut and king salmon during the week they spent with us.

A couple of years later Bob came alone, and as always we enjoyed great times fishing and jaw-boning. We had a lot in common.

A nice catch of Pacific Cod from home in Kodiak.

Bob was about a year younger than me, had never smoked at all, and never drank, but his kidneys began to shut down in 2014. He had a dialysis machine in his home and used it with increasing frequency. After several serious surgeries, much discomfort, and rapidly diminishing physical abilities he told me in mid-July that as he could no longer hunt, go fishing, drive a motor vehicle, or even walk, he planned to pull the plug on the dialysis machine and his life.

I told Bob that knowing and associating with him had greatly enhanced my life and he was one of the best friends of my lifetime. I'd met him at a hunting show in Vienna, Austria in 1978, so we'd been close friends for thirty-nine years.

Bob said he'd meet me on the "other side" and would have all the good fishing holes and hunting spots figured out to share with me, so I'd waste no time looking.

A few days after our last visit, on July 31, 2017, Bob Penfold passed away and crossed over to the "other side". I miss him.

The Amazon

1988 Bolivia
Preparations

In 1986, while attending a hunting convention in the Midwest, I met a fellow who said he had a brother-in-law who was having problems with jaguars killing too many of his cattle in Bolivia. This sounded like something that might work for me, having essentially most of the time between mid-October and early August free. I got the fellow's address and we began to correspond. The following year, the rancher, Mark, came to the Safari Club International annual convention in Las Vegas, Nevada. After some discussion we agreed that I would travel down to Bolivia, survey the situation, and if feasible, set up a hunting business. Mark had several large ranches, each with infrastructure adequate for a bush hunting operation. He was an American citizen, who had been living in Bolivia since the mid-1960s. It sounded to me like he went south to avoid the draft, but I left that unsaid. He brought the skin of a large male jaguar to the SCI show. I told him that was foolish and dangerous, as it was illegal to import those skins or parts to the USA. I said it would be necessary to jump through all the governmental hoops to keep our business going and, as it involved Jaguars, a restricted species, it would surely be subject to close scrutiny.

Prior to my departure for Bolivia, I obtained from Safari Club International a letter stating that Jaguars taken in Bolivia would be accepted as taken in North America, for those members of SCI who were applying for their "North American 27" recognition. This prestigious

The Amazon

award was given to hunters who legally took at least one of each of the then-recognized 27 big game species of North America. I figured the hunting fraternity "high rollers" would pay plenty for an opportunity to collect a wild Jaguar. We would have to set up a safe operation for our hunting guests. I figured we'd start at $12,000 per hunt. A Brown Bear hunt in Alaska at that time was $6,000 to $8,000.

Importation of Jaguar skins or body parts was illegal in the US at the time, so I arranged for an excellent taxidermist in Germany to receive the hides and skulls, have them tanned, prepare them for the hunter, and store them until importation to the U.S. became legal.

Having heard tales of Vampire bats infecting humans and livestock with rabies, I got injections in Tucson, to immunize me against that most dreaded disease. And it was a good thing I did, as I did see vampires that landed near our horses' hooves, then crawled up the leg far enough to draw blood which they lapped up with their tongues. A common practice of horsemen in Bolivia was to build a small smudge fire to discourage bats and insects. The horses would stand with their noses in the smoke, but their feet and legs were left vulnerable and were commonly exploited by the vampires.

Things were pretty well set up for this new business endeavor, it seemed.

I'd been back in "the States" only about 10 days, after returning from Zimbabwe and South Africa. During that brief stay in the country I did a Shooting and Hunting Sports Fair show north of Phoenix, at the Black Canyon Shooting Range for Dick Haldeman, Bob's (President Nixon's man) brother got my taxes, licenses, etc. straightened out, in preparation for a prolonged trip of six weeks or more to Bolivia, the object of which was to explore the feasibility of setting up a Jaguar hunting operation for me to operate during the long Alaskan winters.

In the interim, I stayed in my camper at my Uncle Stan Nason's place, near Tucson. One evening we rented a Robert Duval movie titled "Let's Get Harry". It's a thriller about an American, named Harry, kidnapped by Colombian rebels and eventually rescued by guys from Harry's midwest hometown. My uncle asked if I was sure I wanted to go "down there". I had some misgivings about it, but I was committed to the trip.

My 1988 Passport picture

As usual, I packed my aluminum trunk with the most critical items, including one of my drillings, this one was a 7X57 rifle with a quick disconnect scope, under a double-barreled 16 gauge shotgun.

The Amazon

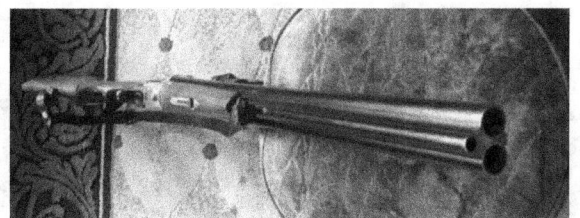

The Drilling was great in close quarters.

A friend of mine, the old Arizona lion, bear and jaguar hunter, C.J. Prock, had emphasized that I should never consider Jaguars to be in the same category as Mountain Lions. He knew that I had crawled down into a cave-like crevasse and shot a large male Arizona cougar through one of its nostrils with a .22 caliber pistol, killing it instantly.

He told me "Jake, them lions is bluffers, as you found out, but I ain't never seen no Jaguar to bluff. They'll try to kill you and they's a strong likelihood that with only a .22 pistol in your hand, they likely gonna be successful."

So, planning to put buckshot in the right barrel, a slug in the left barrel, and a hollow point rifle bullet in the 7X57, I figured I should be able to stop most anything short of a rhinoceros, a hippopotamus, an elephant, or a tank. I packed in some bird shot shells as well, in anticipation of varying my diet options while chasing the bigger game.

From our sole Alaskan US Congressman, Don Young, I got a "Letter of Introduction and Friendship" to carry, just in case problems should arise with customs or police. An old friend from grade school in Arizona was also serving in the U.S. Congress, so I got a similar letter from him. It was written in English and Spanish. I felt pretty well-armed - all the way around, or so I thought at the time.

My itinerary was to depart from Tucson in late March, stop briefly in Dallas, then Miami, and finally in Santa Cruz, Bolivia after a short stop in Panama. I'd checked my two luggage pieces - the trunk and an apple box with rubber boots, rain poncho, etc. only to Miami to be sure that they got on the plane to Bolivia with me. I nearly missed the weekly flight to Santa Cruz due to a temporary loss of the trunk, but, I did make the flight, by the skin of my teeth! It was just plain lucky that my trunk made the same flight.

C.J. Prock and his wife, Dorothy, seated amidst Jaguar trophies, after a meal of fried chicken and oysters - his favorite.

En route, I struck up a conversation with an attractive young lady who was going to Santa Cruz to visit her fiancé' who was working for a U.S. oil company in the area. She was anxious that her man might not meet her and that she would be alone in that very different and foreign land. Hearing her concerns, I assured her that, in the unlikely event that he was not there to meet her, I would see to her safety and comfort.

The Amazon

Before landing I reviewed my Passport and read the letters of Introduction and Friendship from the Alaskan Congressman and then that of the Arizona Congressman. I had not carefully proofread the second one and was appalled to read that the Arizona Congressman's staff had referred to me as an Arizona resident. That, I feared, might cause some confusion for Bolivians and grief for me. I should have shredded that second letter and dumped it, but unfortunately, I did not.

Very soon, my inaction would prove to be a serious mistake.

I planned to fly to Santa Cruz, then by surface transportation along the Grande River to the Beni district. From there we would travel by small boats.

OFF SEASON PURSUITS

POLICE PROBATION, INTERPOL

When we secured our baggage, we were routed through the local customs officials. The ornery little fellow who came to inspect my luggage was feisty and rude from the onset.

This customs official had never before seen a three-barreled gun like the Drilling I brought, and he was concerned about some radio crystals and outboard motor parts that the rancher had asked me to bring for him. He was rude and overly officious as he searched my aluminum trunk, but then he produced a switchblade knife with a blade about six inches long and began to cut open sealed packages of sugar-free mints and chewing gum, which I carried along on most of my foreign trips to give to the children that I would likely encounter. The contents of these packages spilled on the floor and as I began to bristle, the "inspector" thrust his knife into the apple box which contained my rubber boots, rain poncho, and other items that I figured were of lesser importance and/or could be replaced in Bolivia.

Surely, now my gear was no longer waterproof.

Having recently departed Africa, where in those days, if a black government official should become too "cheeky", a few words of aggressive verbal outrage by a white person would usually result in a submissive "Yes, Boss" from the black official, I grabbed the forearm of the Bolivian official's knife hand and said in Spanish " I don't like your manners with the knife, call your boss !" (No me gusta su manera con cuchillo, llama su superior!") The problem was, this guy was the boss! He emitted a shrill whistle and the command "Venga ", to which three large, and well-armed uniformed, police responded. I was roughly ushered into a small side room, accompanied by the three uniformed police and the inspector. The door was slammed shut and two of the "Police" began tearing my clothes off. Buttons flew, I was thrust face-first into a bare wall, one of the men hit me once over my right kidney and I was on the floor in agony. I assure the reader that having one's clothes torn off by aggressive strangers in a smalll closed rom is a very intimidating situation. The kidney punch confirmed my sense of peril.

Obviously, resistance was not in order at that time, but I decided that if I could get hold of one of the automatic weapons carried by each of the uniformed men, I would endeavor to kill everyone in the room. It seemed at the time that my chances of surviving this situation were minimal, and were decreasing with every passing moment.

The four men in the small room with me were talking rapidly in Spanish and I gathered that they were feeling extremely hostile toward me and had little to be concerned about regarding how they treated me.

The little man, the "jefe" or head man, came in with my passport and the two letters of Introduction and Friendship. He was jabbering, loud and irritated! He had an interpreter read the material and the discrepancy about my residency immediately came to light. My identification and one letter attested to me being an Alaskan resident, but the letter from the Arizona congressman stated that I was a resident of that state.

He was convinced that I was a criminal and asked about more passports or identifying documents. To his way of thinking, he had iron-clad proof of my guilt.

A soft knock on the door froze the action. The supervisor cautiously opened the door and there stood the rancher, Mark, who was to have met me about 20 minutes earlier. My assailants knew this American, treated him with great respect, and permitted him to enter the room as he told them that I was a friend (amigo, un caballero) and not a mercenary or drug runner and he would vouch for me and put up a financial bond if necessary, as he needed me for some serious veterinary projects that were to commence at one of his remote estancias within days.

Mark kept the supervisor engaged in a pleasant banter as the two moved out of the room and I was left with the three armed, glowering men in the tiny room. Their fun was interrupted, and they were not happy about that ! Shortly thereafter, another uniformed man opened the door and told me to dress myself. He motioned to the others to come with him. My shirt was torn and buttons were all over the floor, so clothed or not, I looked like a disheveled mess.

Mark explained to me that my luggage would be held and I would have to report to the downtown Santa Cruz police station daily until my identity could be verified and it was ascertained that I did not have a record with Interpol.

What? I thought Interpol only existed in mystery novels.

As we departed the terminal, I caught a glimpse of the young lady whose safety and comfort I had offered to defend. She did not make eye contact with me, but sat on a wooden bench, waiting, and hoping, no doubt, for her fiancé. The inspector gave me a penetrating stare, steeped in malevolence. I stepped into the hot, humidity which waited for everyone outside the terminal. I noticed the odor of many unwashed, sweaty humans.

It occurred to me later that Mark may well have delayed meeting me to allow me to see the danger of the police and the influence he had with them.

Once in Mark's Toyota pickup, he opened the glove box and handed me a holstered .357 Magnum revolver. I told him that I wanted nothing to do with that, as it seemed I was already in trouble with the local police. He said for me to take it and that I should not even go to the toilet without it. "This is the wild west", he said. "With no pistola, escopeta (shotgun), or rifle, you get no respect." He did add that it would not be a good idea to carry it on my person to my daily downtown police visits.

We stopped in a small store and got a couple of quarts of cold local Pilsner beer which was very good and most welcomed by me.

Mark was proud to show me some jaguar skins his workers had brought to him - all were killed on one or another of his remote ranch properties.

Mark's villa (or finca) on the edge of town was very nice. A large brick manor house sat on a hill about 20 feet higher than the surrounding flat chaparral. A barn, garage, and various other smaller structures - a chicken house, goat pen, etc.- were located about 50 meters from the owner's home. An employee came out to greet Mark, but I detected a resigned tolerance, rather than affection for Mark from his employee.

Inside, the cook and housekeeper greeted me warmly and Mark told his cook to prepare some appetizers. In the meantime, he took me to his office where he showed me a local newspaper with his picture on the front page. He told the story of how one dark night, in that same room, he, his wife, and their two young sons had been held at gunpoint by three men, one with a pistol, and the others wielding butcher knives. He said the villains told him that they would kill his family, then him, unless he opened his safe and gave them the money they knew was inside. It was common practice in Bolivia for employers like Mark to keep cash on hand for paying their workers.

Apparently, to make the threat credible, one of the fellows with a knife cut the side of Mark's wife's neck and struck her with the butt of the knife, knocking her to the floor. The children began crying and Mark agreed to open the safe - pronto.

Under extreme stress, Mark missed on his first two attempts to open the combination lock, but by the third try, he had gathered a calm resolve and as the last pin fell, he opened the heavy door, grabbed his 9 mm Walther pistol, turned quickly and shot the pistolero in the forehead, killing him instantly. He hit one of the other men in the thigh as he ran for the door, but that man and the third would-be robber ran out the door, across the patio, and into the moonless night.

The sound of the pistol shots had aroused several workers who had been playing cards in their quarters near the garage. They all came to the main house calling for Mark and asking if he was "seguro".

Mark told the men to call others from nearby fincas to help catch these bad guys and get the dogs and their handler on the fresh trail, but to hold off on calling the police.

Before many neighboring men had arrived, Mark's crew had brought the wounded man's body into the yard - his femoral artery had been severed by the shot and he had already bled to death. His untouched accomplice was tied up and lying in the driveway in front of the main house. He was crying and pleading that he was not responsible for the attempted robbery.

Mark ordered that his Toyota pickup be brought to him. The tied man began to beg, but when the truck arrived, Mark got in it and repeatedly drove over the chest of the man, killing him. There were no protests from those in attendance. Then Mark called the police. In describing the incident as I have told here, the newspapers made a hero of Mark. Obviously people believed in ending and preventing future bad behavior. It seemed reasonable to me.

Justice had come swiftly and at no cost to society at large.

Shortly thereafter, Mark's wife and children returned to the U.S. where she said they would remain.

We enjoyed a well-prepared meal of Bolivian beef, potatoes, fresh salad, and banana pie.

My sleep was interrupted several times by unfamiliar sounds and disturbing dreams, but as usual, I was up before daylight, in time to see what appeared to be a small grey fox - a zorro gris - dart off the patio and into the nearby scrub.

The next evening I shot the beautiful male grey fox with a .22.

The Amazon

Mark was in his office at the single-sideband HF radio, checking in with his various enterprises in the bush. He made notes as he conversed in Spanish. He waved me in for a cup of hot coffee - Nescafe, it was. I wondered about the use of instant coffee in a tropical locale suitable for growing the beans, but Nescafe seemed to be the norm in Bolivia. The housekeeper brought in a hearty breakfast of bacon, eggs, toast, and sliced oranges and we were soon off to Santa Cruz in the Toyota pickup.

My daily appointment with the local Police was scheduled for 10 am. As we were in town well before that, we stopped at the home of a most interesting fellow who spoke German and Spanish. Max claimed to be a Belgian, who arrived in Bolivia in 1945. (About the time that a lot of Germans arrived in that part of the world, on the run from the allies in Europe.) Max was an all-around handy fellow and proved to be very knowledgeable in mechanics, hunting, fishing, and all manner of jungle bushcraft. We visited over another Nescafe, then Mark told Max of his plan to go to Rondonia, the Brazilian Province set aside for the indigenous, primitive Indians.

Max produced a newspaper article with photographs of the bodies of two surveyors, each with several long arrows projecting from their chest and abdomen. These men had become separated from their main group and had come to their untimely end in the same area of the reserve we were planning to visit. The article was dated early March 1988. It was less than a month old.

Max then told us of his previous encounters with the "wild ones" (Salvajes) and reminded us that if we saw any people not with our party in the deep jungle of Rondonia, we were to shoot them as soon as possible - before they could shoot us. I had reservations about doing that, but I kept my thoughts to myself, and hoped I would not be faced with such a situation.

An agreement was made and Max assured Mark that he would begin welding up some suitable boats, getting enough other equipment, outboard motors, a generator, a small chest freezer, and personnel to make the trip. He planned to bring along two of his sons, plus a nephew, and hire others as we passed through the Beni district of Bolivia, which shared a border with Brazil.

Mark drove me to the Police station, where I waited in line in the sun, along with rough-looking street whores, pickpockets, perpetrators of various crimes, people involved in traffic accidents, and other wrongdoers, for my "appointment". It seemed no preference was given to the severity of the alleged crime. By the time I was summoned to the desk of the chief, about two and a half hours later, I was wringing wet from sweat which oozed even faster from my person once I entered the dank outer office. I got only a perfunctory glance, the officer made a note that I had appeared. Then he told me to report again the following day.

Back on the street and free until 10 am the next day, I stopped in a nearby bar to wait for Mark to pick me up. This was in 1988 and no one had cell phones. A liter of cold Pilsner went down easily. Seated at the long bar was a fellow who asked me in good English where I was from. When I said Alaska was home, he said he was from Ketchikan. He had just come down to Bolivia, knocking around, spending some of his fishing money before going back to the north country. As we visited, I mentioned Mark. The fellow from Ketchican cautioned me to be very careful with "that guy". He said that two Americans were rotting in a Santa Cruz jail as we spoke. These men had come to work for, or with, Mark, but after a considerable time working, they asked to be paid and found themselves in jail on vague charges. He told me that he understood that they had been jailed about three months ago and did not have a court or release date. I mentally filed that information along with some of my recent observations that gave me pause to consider whether or not I should just get the okay from the police and then fly back to Arizona. I devoured some bar appetizers as I deliberated. Memories of the movie "Let's Get Harry" troubled my thoughts.

Mark showed up about mid-afternoon and took me to a lumber supply to pick up an order for one of his ranches. We were greeted and taken into a lavish office. The owner was most gracious and offered us to help ourselves to a pile of white powder on his desk. I figured it was cocaine. We both declined.

As we drove back to the Finca, Mark said that refined cocaine was readily available in any city, but most locals did not use it. Nearly everyone chewed coca leaves, even students and truck drivers used it, as it helped them fight drowsiness, but the refined powder was just for gringos. I told him that I had never sampled cocaine and I had no interest in doing so, even if it were free.

The remainder of the afternoon was spent with Mark checking various projects at the Finca, the home garden, work on some vehicles, a new perimeter fence with the latest security features, and some work on the road. The main course of the evening meal was Pacu which is probably the most delicious fish I have ever eaten. These large, round fish are reportedly fruit eaters, found in rivers beneath fruit trees, erupting to strike pieces of fruit as they fall into the water. Mark had rum and coke while I downed a couple of gin and tonics. I slept much better than I had on the first night.

The next morning I awoke to the housekeeper's gentle call that breakfast was ready. After the meal, I asked Mark to drop me off at the Police station as early as possible, in hopes of avoiding the long line and perhaps going to Max's to help, or at least observe the boat construction. I had a book to read. Though I was first in line, the chief took others ahead of me - I was the only gringo - but still, I received his nod and was finished just before noon. I went back to the bar for a cold Pilsner and perhaps more information from the Alaskan fisherman, but he was not in the bar that day, and I did not see him again.

The welds all looked excellent.

A cab to Max's put me at his gate just in time for their midday meal, in which I partook. It was good fare, with lots of poultry, red meat, rice, and yucca - a starchy staple in that part of the world. The three boats were already taking shape. Constructed of corrugated metal roofing, reinforced with flat and angle iron, 12 feet in length, about four and a half feet in width, they appeared stable and river-worthy.

Max's parrot was not put off by the noisy work, not even the welding, but continued its croaky banter, in spite of being largely ignored by the busy crew. I noticed the powerful beak and curved talons and decided to not attempt a friendship with the large bird, though it grabbed at my sandal straps and hectored me for attention. Max's daughter and the younger children got a big laugh at me, the gringo who didn't want to hold their parrot.

On day four, after making my appearance at the Police station in Mark's Toyota pickup, as I drove along a tree-lined street I noticed a pretty girl walk by me. About a half block up the street she walked past some young men seated on a bench. As she drew near, one of the men stood and grabbed her by the arm. She resisted, trying to get away. I drove the Toyota up onto the sidewalk and got out, asking what the problem was. The man holding the girl told me in Spanish to mind my own business, at which I told him in Spanish to let her go or I would break his arm.

"Deja su bravo o voy a romper lo tuyo" I declared.

His two companions stood up as I walked briskly toward them. The first man released the girl with some negative comments for me - actually, he roundly cussed me out - but he backed up.

"Piensas que puede romper my bravo,eh?" (You think you can break my arm.) He blurted.

"Estoy listo a mostrarte," (I'm ready to show you) was my reply.

I did not answer his insults. I offered the young woman a ride, but she refused, so, as she walked at a brisk pace, I idled alongside the walkway in the pickup, until she paused at a fenced yard, thanked me, and went inside. I got out of the truck as the young woman and a slightly older woman came out of the house. I introduced myself and asked if I might come by to visit in the near future.

Demurely, the younger one said, "Perhaps". Then she gave me her telephone number.

This young lady was uniquely pretty. I could not get her off my mind. I wrote down the address and phone number.

After 5 days of diligently reporting to the Police station, word finally arrived from Interpol that I was not a known revolutionary, drug trafficker, or terrorist - at least I wasn't on their list. The chief delivered the news to me but raised his eyebrow as if to indicate that he was not completely convinced. As Mark had suggested, I discretely placed two twenty-dollar bills in the palm of my armed and unformed escort as we walked down the hallway. Then I was taken to an evidence room where my aluminum trunk and apple box luggage with all their contents were returned to me.

I took my good news back to Max's shop where work on the boats had progressed to the point of coating the bottoms with a thick tar-like material that when dried, was tough and smooth. Without this protective coating, the "tin" boats would rust through in a few weeks, I was told.

Mark produced a letter from the President of Bolivia, which though written on very official appearing stationary, I suspected to be fabricated. Hunting was forbidden in Bolivia, but this letter gave its bearer and his party a carte blanche for collecting any game, insects, plants, and most anything else they came upon. A small chest freezer was delivered that afternoon which was to run off of the gas generator already sitting in Max's shop. We were nearly ready for the big trip. I was relieved at not being detained longer by the police which could have kept me from making that trip!

After a light noon meal followed by a short siesta, we all walked around the corner to attend the local cock fights. I'd never before seen such aggressive chickens. In some cases, it was a fight to the death. Wagering was enthusiastic and noisy, but amidst the great emotion generated by the fowl combatants, the human spectators and bird handlers maintained a surprising civility. There seemed to be no drinking at this "sporting" event.

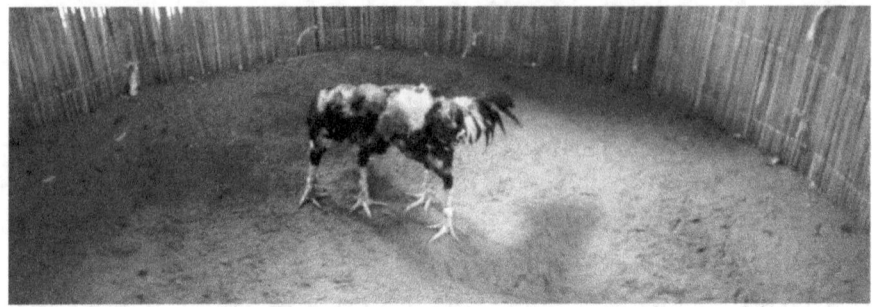

Two roosters seriously going at it.

That evening I called the pretty girl, Teresa, whom I'd met the day before, and asked if she would be interested in taking an ice cream with me at the shop near her residence. She said she would ask her sister. Approval was given, so I was at her doorstep at 7:00 pm. I left the truck parked as we walked to the sweet shop. Ice cream was a favorite in this area and the locally made stuff, "helados", was very good. Teresa was enrolled in college, pursuing a degree in Fashion Design and Styling, she explained to me.

On our way to the ice cream parlor.

I am about as fashion-conscious as an on-the-job truck mechanic and had never paid much attention to style, either, but my attention was focused on her She was truly alluring. I explained that in a few days, I would be going on an extended trip of unknown duration, into the jungle in search of hunting opportunities, which might be such that I would be spending winters in that area while my Arctic hunting areas were in the annual deep freeze. She seemed fascinated with my stories of walking for miles on natural snow, the giant deer we call Moose, my two "tractors" which were Honda 110s and other things common to Arctic Alaska.

It seemed the day of departure arrived too soon. We loaded three trucks, three boats, and a trailer and crossed the Rio Grande near Santa Cruz, bound for the Beni district. At that point, we numbered seven men, Mark, Max, two of his sons, one nephew, a young neighbor man, and myself.

Ox carts were in common use throughout Bolivia and South America

RONDONIA

Ox carts outnumbered petroleum powered vehicles and had less trouble in the near quicksand conditions of the river bed. They were slow, sure, and no sweat. The road was dirt, but not too dusty. It seemed that every two hours or so we would come upon a collection of shops, mostly small eateries clustered alongside the road, chicken, pork, and pan- fried bread were the most common menu items. In that muggy heat, some of the shops' fare smelled spoiled, so I often deferred, able to survive in reasonable comfort with my granola bars, bread, jerky, and fresh fruit.

I had some dull back pain in my right kidney area, probably from the policeman's single punch which was irritated by the potholed roads. The pain seemed to increase the overall discomfort of my situation. I tried to ignore it.

Two days of driving the potholed, dusty road with a six to eight-hour evening stop put us at the river launching site. As two of the younger men made camp for the night I roamed around in the bush. The vegetation was dense, but easily cleared with a machete. I'd tried using a machete on Alaskan willow and alder, but those tough northern plants just sprang back, often slapping me in the face. I'd long since gone to using a Swede saw, pruning shears, or an ax to clear paths in the north. I was struck by the fact that in spite of the heat, I felt energized. Could it be that the oxygen produced by all the vegetation caused it, or was it my level of excitement?

The first bushmaster I killed crossing the road at sundown.

As I hacked my way through dense brush I was reminded of the thumbless "chicleros" I'd met in Belize two years before. A common injury to users of machetes, including those harvesting chicle plants is the loss of the thumb of the hand holding whatever thing is to be hacked. I tried to keep this ever in mind while using a machete. I was amazed at how effective the big knife was on these tropical stalks.

When I returned the hammocks were hung with mosquito nets in place and chicken was being grilled on the coals. Yucca and stick bread completed the fare, washed down with some very fine, mild, but, this time, insufficiently chilled, Pilsner beer.

Shortly after dark, we were all asleep.

Early the next morning we launched the three small boats and set off for the wilds of Rondonia.

With the chest freezer, electric generator, and all the hunting, fishing, and camping gear we were crowded, but tolerably comfortable.

After not more than three hours of slow travel, we came upon a collection of tents and people on the river bank. Two men with AK47 assault rifles were standing on the bank near some tents and motioned us to come to them. They did not look friendly.

Max engaged them in conversation and went ashore, escorted by one of the men. The others remained, watching us closely, their automatic firearms at the ready.

Mark mentioned that we all should remain very docile and not do anything to alarm the guard. After thirty minutes, Max returned with three other guards, all armed with AK47s. Max was carrying a bag which he tossed into his boat and with friendly farewells to the guards, he told us to shove off and continue up the river without looking back.

We are stopped at a riverside cocaine camp.

At our next stop, Max told me that was the first of many cocaine processing camps that we would encounter. He knew one of the local superintendents from previous trips on the river and the fellow had offered him a bag of coca leaves, which he accepted. He offered some to us and we all had a chew. Coca leaves serve as a mild stimulant, helping to combat drowsiness, but do not cause the euphoria reported to follow the use of refined cocaine. These mini "refineries" were well known and tolerated by locals. They were an important source of cash income. The refined product was for export only and not in common use by residents. These leaves, as we chewed them would not become destined for widespread, international use.

We passed several more similar camps without incident, other than being asked to come ashore, allowing close scrutiny of us by the drug camp officials. Max assured the operators that we posed no threat to them.

A White Piranha biting a stick.

The three boats made of corrugated roofing tin performed well on the muddy Amazon tributary. All the streams were muddy.

After four days of travel, we arrived at the first place from which Max intended to hunt. Here, we unloaded the chest freezer and put it in the more substantial and comfortable camp. Immediately the "boys" were throwing out baited fishing lines and soon had a very colorful catfish weighing over 30 pounds. Piranha were also abundant, with tasty white flesh. We were happy to eat them and relieved that it was not the other way around.

Night hunts produced several "Hochis", small rodents called Agoutis in Central America, which were also very tasty eating.

A verly tasty Amazon catfish.

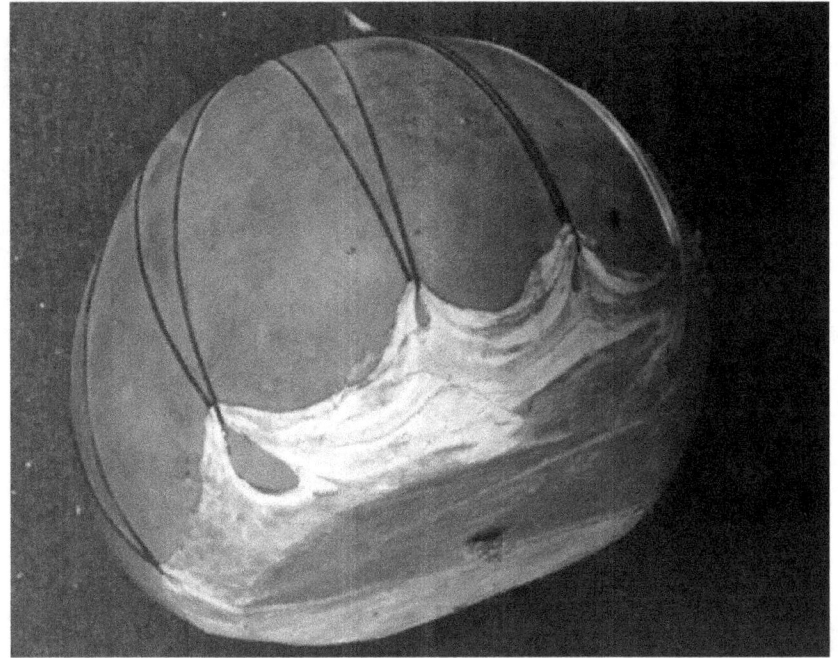
A "Llama Tigre" gourd for calling Jaguars.

From one of the Indians helping us, I traded two shotgun shells for a "Llama Tigre" or Jaguar call made from a hollow gourd with a piece of deer stomach laced across the large hole on one end, from which a tarred string hung into the inside. By gently pulling the string, a rasping sound like that made by a rutty Leopard or Jaguar was produced. It proved to be effective in bringing male Jaguars into conversation.

I'm holding two smaller Pacu fish with four Hochi rodents from the previous night's hunt, ready to butcher.

One night one of the Indians, called Indio, who had a very nasty scar running from his forehead, across the socket of one blinded eye, and into his cheek, and I were in a dug-out canoe, drifting, calling, then moving on to call from another location. After about an hour of trying to entice a Jaguar we were conversing with into a position allowing me a clear shot, Indio said abruptly that we had to go, immediately and he untied the bow line and began to paddle us into the middle of the stream, catching the current and heading down river and toward our camp.

This fellow was very rough-looking and no doubt had lived a violent, dangerous life, but I had confidence in him and did not question his actions.

Ashore in camp Indio asked me in Spanish (none of the "boys" spoke English) if I smelled the "Sikuri"? I said that I had noticed a musky order, similar to what I had smelled on rattlesnakes (caskabels in the local dialect) in Arizona during August.

"Si, Si, era un sikuri, pienso que era un grande - cerquita" Which translates to "Yes, yes, it was an Anaconda, I think a big one, close by." In the dugout on a river populated by piranha, alligators, caiman, and who knows what else, a large Anaconda could easily tip us out into the river which would not be a desirable situation, full of dangerous potential consequences. I was relieved to see that he was not into taking undue chances.

The locals feared the Sikuri more than any other wild animal in the jungle or river. Jaguars or Tigres are the next most feared.

One evening after the meal, my kidney pain became nearly intolerable. One of the customs police at the airport had delivered a very effective kidney punch to my right side and I attributed my recurring pain in that area to internal damage caused by his fist. I'd had a kidney stone in 1977, eleven years before, and I knew the feeling all too well. I was in the grip of dull, but severe pain. Periodic episodes lasted for up to fifteen minutes. I felt nauseated each time I had such an episode. I always dreaded having such an attack while flying an airplane, but, thank God, that never happened

Indio made a puree of green bananas and coca leaves which he rubbed on the small of my back and told me to chew a big wad of the leaves. After an hour, I felt much better, but my urine showed bright red blood. The "treatment" was apparently successful as my pain was minimal, but my bloody urine persisted intermittently for several days.

Off Season Pursuits

One of our jungle overnight camps on a riverbank in Rondonia.

Guan, a type of jungle fowl - that evening's wildfowl dinner to be.

The hunting and fishing efforts were producing results. We were eating very well, dining on the most exotic fare imaginable. Every day was a new adventure for me. And many nights were, too!

One evening as we all sat around the campfire, roasting some Guan, or wild jungle fowl, I noticed a large snake coming into the circle of light. Anacondas were bringing about $100 per foot from animal dealers and with my snake-catching experience from Arizona, I decided I would capture that one.

Indio said "No, no patron, cuidado, es un cascabel!" I said it was a Sikuri, as it clearly had no rattles. However, soon after I learned that in the local dialect, cascabel means merely that it is one of several types of venomous pit vipers, with the Bush Master and Fer-de-Lance being the most dangerous. I touched the head of the serpent with a long pole and it struck, showing huge fangs. This was clearly not the behavior I would expect from a constrictor. So I hollered to Indio to bring my shotgun. (Dame mi escopeta).

The snake was not overly active, but definitely seemed agitated and distracted as it tried to keep track of so many people. I was able to shoot it about ten inches behind the head and the serpent began writhing violently with its head nearly severed.

The snake was over ten feet long and the fangs measured over two inches in length. It was a Bushmaster, reported to be the most aggressive and poisonous of all new world snakes, having venom made up of both neurotoxic and proteolytic components. Those large fangs could deliver a potentially lethal dose of venom very deep into its victim's flesh.

This one had just consumed two medium sized rodents and seemed sluggish. No one could explain why it had come so close to us at the camp fire, but all the "boys" were agitated and relieved that it was dead. We skinned it and ate it's stringy white flesh which tasted about like the rattlesnake I had eaten on several occasions in Montana and Arizona. Butter and garlic make it palatable.

Indio told me that this snake species was not known to travel in pairs, unlike the Fer-de-Lance - called Tommygoff in Belize, so we could all sleep soundly, at least for that night.

Skin of the ten-foot Bushmaster, which was larger than the road-killed one, and a small Alligator. We ate both critters.

Each day brought something new. Mosquitos were not nearly as thick here as they are during June and July in Arctic Alaska but these pestiferous insects potentially carried malaria.

Kissing bugs live in that part of the tropics and can lead to a bloodborne organism that eventually ruins the heart of those who have had its lethal kiss. I recorded on film and video some very strange and dangerous-looking insects, but I was not adversely affected by any. Of course, I was taking prophylactic quinine to avoid malaria.

We harvested a Capybara, one Tapir, a dozen "Hochis" (great tasting small rodents of five to fifteen pounds in weight, and with white meat), jungle fowl, ducks, some pheasant-like birds, Grey Brocket Deer, Red Brocket Deer, White Lipped Peccaries, Collared Peccaries, a Coatimundi, several different species of monkeys and many types of fish. The meat of any critter we harvested went into the cook pot, which served like a crockpot.

21 One type of "kissing bug"

Two Hochi Pintao, or Painted Agoutis. Others were "Colorado" with solid reddish-brown pelage.

This Tamandua's tongue was over 16 inches long.

The southern tamandua (Tamandua tetradactyla), also called the collared anteater or lesser anteater is found from Trinidad to Argentina. It has a head and body length ranging from 13 to 35 in, and a prehensile tail 15 to 26 in long. Adults weigh from 3.3 to 18.5 lb, with no significant difference in size between males and females. They have four-clawed digits (tetra dactyla) on the forefeet and five on the hind feet and walk on the outer surfaces of their forefeet to avoid puncturing their palms with their sharp claws.

I've never liked muddy water, but the rivers in this part of the Amazon were always muddy.

And muddy water can produce interesting game. "

Gators or caimen were often enountered - and eaten.

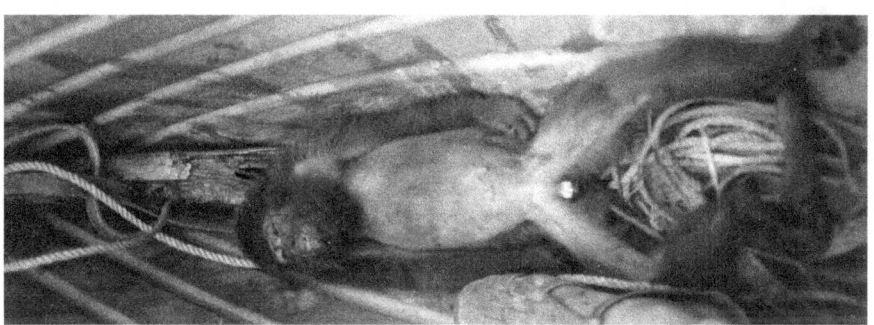

Red Howler monkey was not appetizing,
but, if hungry, and spiced enough, it tastes okay.

A large Pacu, a tasty relative of the piranha.

The most interesting, flavorful, and best-eating fish - perhaps in the world, is the Pacu. I was told that these stout river denizens ate only fruit. We caught them by running a boat underneath a fruit-bearing tree overhanging the river, then we put a small fruit on a large "J" hook which was attached to a 500-pound test parachute cord, and tossed it under the tree. The water would erupt as the fish took the fruit in a jump. Fishermen needed to protect their hands with leather gloves, lest the "fishing line" cut them. I have never eaten more delicious fish flesh.

I asked what the Pacu ate when fruit was out of season and was told "Pero Patron, here, fruit is always in season."

We were spending two to four days and nights in each camp, then moving on. Late one afternoon, about twelve days into the trip, Max and one of the "boys" came back from fishing. They were very excited. Max ordered everyone to pack up, as we must leave as soon as possible. He had found three arrows about fifty-five to sixty inches in length, that he said had been left as a warning near our camp. The savages were near and we had to depart, - immediately. He posted me at the edge of our camp and told me to shoot any savage Indians that I saw, as soon as I saw them, as we were in extreme peril! "Muy peligroso", he emphasized. He repeated that I should not say anything, nor delay, just shoot. With my drilling, I had three quick shots, if needed. I was uncomfortable with the situation and did not care for the thought of just shooting any stranger who showed up. Luckily, such a situation did not develop.

Within thirty minutes we were loaded and ready to shove off. I carefully placed the arrows in "my boat", but Indio said it was bad luck and that I should throw them overboard. I told him that I'd never before seen arrows like these and I planned to take them home.

We traveled downstream until past midnight, then quietly made camp on a small island we'd used earlier that week. The next morning, when we loaded to depart, I noticed that the arrows were no longer in the boat. I figured Indio had dumped them. But I did not mention it to anyone. We traveled several more miles before setting up a more comfortable camp where we stayed for two nights, mostly fishing. Max remained on full alert and finally decided that we'd done well enough and we should go home before any serious trouble developed. I was ready for that.

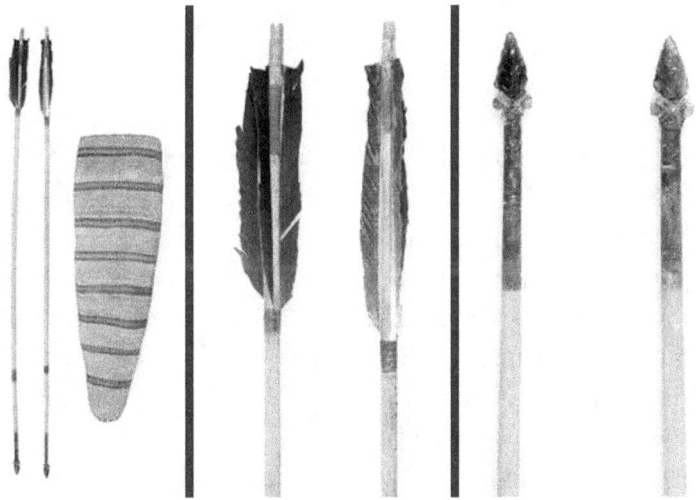

The primitive arrows were about sixty inches in length.

We went back downriver to the vehicles, again being detained at each cocaine "factory" just long enough to ascertain that we seemed to pose no threat. Nevertheless, I was uncomfortable with the situation and the guards having us at such a disadvantage. If an individual decided to do us evil we were completely vulnerable. The two-day return drive to town seemed much slower and more torturous than coming the other way.

Perhaps the most important thing I brought with me from Rondonia was the appreciation of the healing powers of gasoline. Indio cut himself on two occasions. Each time he asked for a small amount of gasoline, with which he dosed and cleaned the cut. His wounds healed within two days, and without a scar! In 2005 in Kodiak, I had a Staphylococcus Aureus infection of a finger for which our physician recommended hospitalization with intravenous Vancomycin, administered through the Inguinal vein, at the cost of $2,500/day, but I refused. That same day I accidentally spilled gasoline from my lawnmower on my infected finger which dramatically reduced the production of the golden pus. After two days and four more "gas ups," the extremely dangerous Staph infection was gone. Since then, I have used gasoline on other cuts ranging from superficial to deep with similar results.

Needless to say, this healing medicine is not to be taken internally!

THE PATANAL

Once back in Santa Cruz Mark began making arrangements to charter a Cessna 206 to one of his estancias, or outback cattle stations. Caraparasito it was called, which sounded to me like "parasite face".

The first station we visited was in the Pantanal, a very lush jungle area with occasional open grasslands. The Cordillera consisted of a range of high hills or low mountains which were thickly forested and punctuated by occasional rocky outcrops. Many streams drained the hills into the predominantly swampy lowlands.

The local headman had sent a radio message that a large male Jaguar was killing cattle in the bush and he wanted some help in dispatching the predator. He suggested that we bring some extra dogs for trailing the cat.

As we flew over the roadless jungle I wondered at the navigational abilities of the pilot with the apparent lack of landmarks, but after an hour's flight, (about 120 miles) suddenly we were over a dirt strip. It was just a narrow open band hacked from the dense brush and mixed forest. This was years before the availability of GPS units to civilians.

After a hearty round of introductions and handshaking, we loaded the carts and started for the estancia located about a kilometer away. Saddle horses were brought for Mark and me.

I was told that the main house was built by the Germans, from whom Mark purchased the station. It showed construction craftsmanship far superior to any other structure in the area. The actual acreage under ownership was uncertain, but I believe it was vast. Nearly a dozen other, lesser stations provided shelter sufficient to satisfy the locals and adequate for short stays by most visitors. Except for periods of torrential rainfall, Mark and I hung our hammocks outside and slept under a mosquitero net at the outback stations.

Two oxcarts were awaiting our arrival. The drivers and a collection of women and children were clustered at the turnaround area on one end of the strip.

Me and Indio with Hammocks slung and mosquiteros in place.

A photo of the most recently killed macho(male) Tigre.

Several Jaguar skins and skulls were tacked upon the interior walls of the main house. We enjoyed a fine meal after which I checked my gear and read a little before going to bed. Mark was up late organizing the trip for the next morning.

Shortly after sunrise, we were on the trail. The hunting party made a long string of horses, Mark and I, and four of his caballeros were mounted, with eight heavily loaded pack horses being led. Most of the day was spent traveling through the dense jungle. Streams that were no more than three or four feet in depth were crossed with riders mounted. On some occasions, we would come to a stream large and deep enough to unload the pack animals and place their burdens into dugout canoes that were available at each crossing. We men, would strip down to our shorts, then swim the river with our mounts swimming just behind. All these activities were done in a matter-of-fact fashion. I wondered silently about the potential danger of Anacondas, Piranhas, or crocodilians, but since no one else mentioned them, I kept my silence on the issue, though I wondered if my whanger might look like food to a Piranha.

Another water crossing.

Off Season Pursuits

When darkness fell, we continued on. I had a small flashlight handy and played its beam around the area, especially in the denser jungle. I was surprised at how many snakes infested that part of the world. Some serpents in the trees and bushes appeared to be white. I got a good look at many of those above ground but only partial sightings of those in the trail ahead. I was relieved to not be walking amidst so many strange serpents.

Just before midnight, we arrived at a bush station. As one of the men with us opened the gate to put the horses in the corral, an employee came from the house with a lantern and greetings. Mark stayed mounted as his horse was led to the shack. Again, I got the distinct feeling that Mark was tolerated and perhaps respected, but not well-liked.

The thought occurred to me that one could easily be knocked in the head, left in the bush, and soon would moulder, be eaten or decompose, leaving no trace. It definitely seemed a better idea to treat people well, in hope and anticipation of similar treatment from them.

One of the bush camp shelters.

Vampire bats are indigenous to that area and at dusk each day, one of the workers would start small smudge fires in the corral, and then place bags over the horses' noses. The horses clustered near the small fires with their heads low, apparently to avoid being fed upon by the bats and insects.

We had some granola bars and jerky, as well as plenty of fresh fruit. When I got a whiff of the meat that had been put out for us that evening, I stayed with our snacks. With no refrigeration available, the meat was often spoiled, but the locals consumed it without a pause or apparent ill effects. I decided to not test my gut on that issue.

The next morning we had some Nescafe and bread before visiting one of the closer Jaguar kill sites. A large steer had been consumed almost completely by a big Jaguar, according to the tracks in the mud. Maggots riddled the remains. Not much was left of the bovine. The smell was reminiscent of that emanating from last night's offering of a beef dinner. In Africa Leopards seem to prefer maggoty meat, as well

The head vaquero said that the kill was three days old and he did not think the Jaguar would return. We rode on to other kills, all of which were badly decomposed and none showed signs of being freshly fed upon.

After some discussion, it was decided to stake out a sickly yearling cow and hope for an opportunity to dispatch the Jaguar. While two of the vaqueros returned to the station to select a cull cow, Mark and I directed (and I helped) the remaining two men to construct a machan or tree platform (a hide) about eight feet above and thirty meters lateral to a small clearing where the bait cow was to be tethered. Within an hour we had built our shooting stand. Insects were extremely pestiferous and no repellant could be used, lest its smell spook the Jaguar. We made a small fire and rubbed ashes on our exposed skin, which helped but was not nearly as effective as a mosquito repellant. I longed for a shower of *Deep Woods Off*.

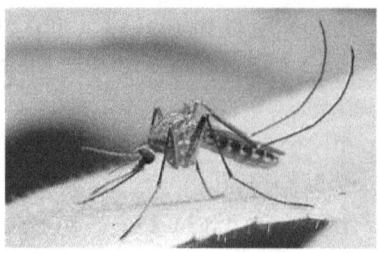

One of the many species of mosquito that fed upon us.

After the sickly-looking heifer was staked out, Mark and three of his men returned to the station, leaving me and a fellow named Manuel to sit through the night for the Tigre.

Insects seemed most ferocious just at dusk, then slacked off after full darkness was upon us. The night sounds were varied and strange to my northern ears. Manuel tried to identify each sound for me, but there were too many unfamiliar ones and I was soon confused. This was going to be a long night.

At about 10:00 pm I heard a distant, raspy ruuugghaaa, which I recognized and knew must be coming from a Jaguar, as it was very similar to that made by African Leopards which I had heard on a few occasions in Southern Rhodesia and Botswana. Manuel immediately whispered, "Tigre, patron Jake, Tigre"!

My drilling had a 7X57 130-grain soft point in the lower barrel, a single ought buckshot in the right shotgun barrel, and a slug in the left tube. The trigger selector was smooth and silent in its operation. I hoped for a very close-range opportunity, at which time I would fire the rifle, then the slug, and then quickly follow with the buckshot.

I gently stroked the string of the Llama Tigre call and waited. The cat answered! Normally the Jaguar made three to five of the "sawing" calls, then was silent for up to twenty minutes. I answered the cat's calls within a minute, then waited. This cat was likely a dominant tom and did not immediately respond to my efforts. I imagined a large male, demonstrating his superiority and authority by his delayed responses.

The big cat toyed with us for more than three hours. He was circling, probably trying to get our scent. At one point, the tethered cow bawled, I was sure the cat was close, which primed me, expecting the cat to make a rush on the cow, but no rush came.

After more than an hour with no calls from the cat, I began to nod, but Manuel's silent nudging kept me from falling asleep. So it went until daylight. The insects became more active with the dawn and our ash treatment had become far less effective as our sweat had diluted it. The poor bait cow looked even worse than when it arrived, but, unfortunately for us, it was untouched, except by insects and a couple of vampire bats.

Two workers came about mid-morning with some breakfast and horses for all. They showed great disappointment at our lack of success and were noticeably twitchy at the prospect of a big cat lurking nearby. I wanted to discuss the situation with Mark, who had remained at the station which was only about 30 minutes by horseback from us. It might be a good idea to have more than one bait station and to inspect the other kill sites well before the evening in order to build at least one more place to hide.

As I prepared to depart, the three vaqueros mounted their steeds to accompany me. I said that two should remain with the bait, but none of them had brought a firearm! And no one was willing to stay behind. Even in full daylight, the locals were terrified of Tigres. Reluctantly I agreed to them coming back with me. I kicked my horse into a rapid walk, breaking into a trot at times, which kept me alert, combating the fatigue from the long night.

Off Season Pursuits

Wading through a mosquito, snake, and Piranha-infested swamp in pursuit of a Jaguar.

Over lunch, Mark and I discussed several options, but with only some .22 pistols, a couple of single-shot .22 rifles, and a badly rusted shotgun at the station, my weapon was the only firearm adequate for use from a blind. So, after a short siesta in my hammock, the three vaqueros and I went back to the bait.

As we neared the clearing I approached cautiously and was shocked to see that the sacrificial cow was gone! It's manilla tether rope was frayed and parted about four feet from the root that had anchored it. We never saw that heifer again. We returned to the station and spent the night in our hammocks.

The jungle horses were small but tough.

Mark thought his dogs would provide us a better chance to kill the cat, so the next morning we set off with nine dogs and seven of us men mounted on horses. I'd hunted cougars in Arizona and New Mexico using hounds which were very effective, but these dogs left a lot to be desired. Not far from the tree stand one dog began to bark and the whole bunch took off into the bush. We haphazardly followed on the horses, but soon lost track of the canines. The foreman pointed out some very fresh appearing Tigre and dog tracks which led into a swamp of knee to waist-deep, stinking, algae-laden water.

Track of the cat next to my 7x57/16ga Drilling.

Three of us waded through the noxious muck to a small palmetto-covered island. The tracks let across the island and into the water on the other side.

From the place where the cat entered the second body of water, I estimated about a half mile to the next elevated area, identified by the stand of palmettos, and decided that following was not going to be worth the effort. However, Manuel did find an armadillo on the island, which he caught alive, and assured me that it would be a wonderful meal, cooked "in the half shell" that evening. During the commotion of catching the armadillo, three of the dogs returned, then led us to another armadillo, which elated Manuel. He kept them alive, as in that heat and humidity, they would spoil quickly if butchered.

When we got back to the horses, Mark was still sitting in his saddle, showing little inclination to continue with the pursuit.

One afternoon while looking for more Jaguar sign, we came across fresh cow tracks. Mark had mentioned that it would be appropriate to slaughter a feral cow for the crew, so I dismounted and followed the tracks into a palmetto thicket. I proceeded very slowly and saw a very good Grey Brocket (Brockets have only spike antlers.) I shot it. It didn't feed as many people as the cow would have done, but this was fresh meat, and delicious.

A Grey Brocket buck we happened upon. Note the deer's huge testicles.

The next day I found this Red Brocket buck brousing nearby

Another "line camp" shelter. In the foreground
- note the home-built cart with wooden wheels.

We spent another week based at the station without ever seeing a Jaguar. Most evenings I and the two or three men assigned to the hunt returned to the station, but we hung our hammocks and mosquiteros outside each night.

If the water was deep, we had to swim across with the horses.

These young "camp girls" fetched us water to bathe, washed our clothes, and performed other chores.

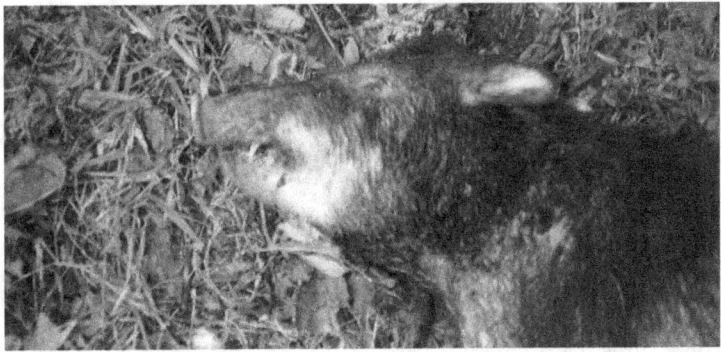

A white-lipped Peccari - the species is a bit larger than the collared Pecarri.

Off Season Pursuits

Our supper was Armadillo and Tortoise,
both served "on the half shell". And both were delicious treats.

These three live Armadillos are destined to be prepared for supper.

But first, I enjoyed the boiled head of Grey Brocket deer.

Armadillos were abundant and eaten often.

During our hunts, a large tortoise was captured and later cooked, as well as several White Lipped Peccarie and some jungle fowl. This wild game was always prepared fresh and was preferred by everyone. The beef that was available quickly became "over-aged" due to the lack of refrigeration. Too often it smelled rotten to me.

A new water craft was hollowed out to cross the large lake.

I was hoping to encounter a Tapir, but I found only this Pecarri.

Bathing with undies left on to avoid tempting
piranhas with our dangling whangers.

When I returned to the states, I went immediately to the local library and looked up Capybara. Genus Hydrochoerus, either of two species of large semiaquatic South American rodents. Capybaras inhabit forests and wetlands from Panama to Argentina. The larger of the two species, the capybara (Hydrochoerus hydrochaeris), is the largest living rodent in the world, growing up to about 1.3 metres (4.3 feet) long and weighing up to 79 kg (174 pounds). The lesser capybara (H. isthmius) is smaller, growing to about 1 metre (about 3 feet) in length and weighing about 28 kg (62 pounds). Some classifications list capybaras as the only members of family Hydrochoeridae, whereas others place them within the subfamily Hydrochoerinae of the family Caviidae. Capybaras resemble the cavy and the guinea pig.

CAPYBARA (HYDROCHOERUS HYDROCHAERIS).

Capybaras are short-haired brownish rodents with blunt snouts, short legs, small ears, and almost no tail. They are shy and associate in groups along the banks of lakes and rivers. They normally feed in the morning and evening and spend most of the day resting under cover along the banks. They are vegetarian and in cultivated areas sometimes become pests by eating melons, grain, and squash. They swim and dive readily and commonly enter water to elude predators such as jaguars and anacondas. The female bears a single litter of three to eight young each year; gestation takes about 100 to 110 days.

The capybara (H. hydrochaeris) occurs in remote areas from Venezuela to northern Argentina and throughout the Amazon River basin. In contrast, the lesser capybara (H. isthmius) is found from central Panama through northwestern Colombia and far northwestern Venezuela. Both forms are considered species of least concern by the International Union for Conservation of Nature and Natural Resources. Capybaras and lesser capybaras are edible and are used for food in various parts of South America: the smaller species is often hunted, whereas the larger species is typically ranched for meat and the animals' hides, which are made into leather goods.

So after twelve days of unsuccessful efforts, due primarily to our lack of experience and poor quality dogs, when the Cessna arrived, we boarded and flew back to Santa Cruz without having taken a Jaguar. A beautiful Ocelot had been treed near the station and shot with a .22 during one of our day trips. It was apparent to me that any wild animal was considered to be fair game by the locals. The small cat's skin was offered to me, but I politely declined as they were not legal to take into the United States. The flesh of the cat was prepared for dinner one evening and reminded me of that of a wild turkey or Alaskan lynx.

With only a few days remaining before I was scheduled to return to Miami, I called Teresa and took her to dinner, then to the ice cream shop. I suggested that she might enjoy a trip to Alaska, to cook for the lodge and perhaps get some schooling. She was interested but told me that getting a Visa would be difficult. I told her that I was sure it could be done and I would accompany her to the Consular Agent the next day.

We drove past the police station where I had been forced to appear daily until I was cleared by Interpol. I did not stop by to say hello.

The United States Consular Agent in Santa Cruz, Bolivia was a middle-aged, chain-smoking, unattractive, caucasian American woman married to a Bolivian man. She displayed a very imperious demeanor, letting us sit and sweat in the muggy waiting room for over an hour as she enjoyed her coffee, cigarettes, and position of authority, in her air-conditioned office. When we were admitted she immediately showed a dislike for Teresa, no doubt due to the fact that Teresa was so young and attractive, attributes with which the agent had never been blessed or had lost due to age. She told me that a cash deposit of $1,700 would ensure that she gave the Visa proper attention. I told her that I had become accustomed to paying "mordida" (bribes) in Bolivia, but not to U.S. officials, and that letters from two U.S. Congressmen would arrive within ten days, which would allow her to proceed with the issuance of the Visa. I also told her that neither I nor the Congressmen would tolerate delays or anything but prompt, professional service. The agent bristled at being spoken to this way and abruptly dismissed us. Teresa was certain that no Visa would be forthcoming.

My kidney stone attacks were by then reoccurring about every ten days or so. When I returned to Tucson, I visited a physician, but no evidence of a stone appeared. He suggested that I be patient and expect the episodes to become less frequent and eventually disappear.

As soon as I got back, I made calls to the two U.S. Congressmen who had given me letters of Introduction for my trip to Bolivia. I described the meeting I had with the Consular Agent and asked that they send letters supporting the issuance of a Visa for Teresa. Both assured me that it would be done, in fact, they gave me copies of telegrams to the agent, advising that letters were in the mail. I expected that would expedite the Visa, but after six weeks, Teresa had not received it.

Well, Teresa had told me it would not be easy.

Our Alaskan Congressman put me in touch with one of his staff, who went by the name of "Tiger". This retired U.S. Army general aggressively pursued the matter with the agent. After several weeks of delays, the agent informed Tiger that Teresa's paperwork had been lost. Tiger was on the telephone immediately and harangued the agent, mentioning that only two Visa applications had been processed by her office in the past six months and she had damned well better locate

Teresa's or face serious repercussions. The Visa was issued the next day and Teresa was soon in Alaska.

In the meantime, Tiger made a trip to Santa Cruz to visit the Consular Agent and gave her notice that her employment had been terminated and the Santa Cruz office was to be closed, permanently. He told me that he mentioned to the Agent that federal employees were not allowed to demand or accept bribes, no matter which country they were assigned. She denied asking for money.

Now, that seemed appropriate punishment for any American official who was demanding private bribes to do the job they were already being well paid for. Formal prosecution should have followed.

My kidney attacks continued until I visited a previous hunting guest of mine who was a physician in Germany. In January 1989 he arranged for me to receive some sonic and other therapy treatments over the course of a week. My painful attacks ended and I have not had any such episodes since then. And I Thank God for that.

By any standards, my sojourn in South America had been the greatest adventure in my life to date. I carried back with me a collection of indelible memories, some fine trophies, and video film ..... and a damaged right kidney.

When Teresa arrived in Anchorage the following August, my old friend, Jim Cann, met her and got her on the next day's plane to Kotzebue.

Teresa adapted well to the far north.

Teresa enjoys the Aufis Glacier on our
80 acres 160 miles north of the Arctic Circle.

Teresa is an excellent cook and companion. In 1993 we married. Teresa gave birth to our daughter Bess in 1994 and to Kate in 1995. I had permanently secured the best part of the Amazon.

EPILOG: BOOK 11

Trips to remote parts of the world are not without risk. My wife and I faced risks in Rhodesia in 1982 when we were confronted with armed, hostile militants, who were likely part of, or in league with, Mugabe's Fifth Brigade.

In the Amazon, we faced numerous risks daily from many sources. Upon my arrival in Santa Cruz, Bolivia, I was forcibly stripped and punched over my right kidney. That caused me pain for several weeks. Among the daily risks were anacondas and venomous snakes, piranha fish, jaguars, and people involved in the cocaine trade.

Physical risk was ever present, considering the animals and places we were hunting or filming.

Sometime after our return to Alaska and my marriage to Teresa, she presented us with two lovely daughters, Bess and Kate.

With their arrival, I had my children's Dad to be concerned about. In addition to my concern for our children - and being uncomfortable with them being raised by only a single parent, I enjoyed just being home with my family. My big foreign travels diminished and came to an end. But our family of four did visit Mexico, Hawaii, Europe, Australia and Tasmania.

www.ingramcontent.com/pod-product-compliance
Lightning Source LLC
Chambersburg PA
CBHW071849230426
43671CB00012B/2115